BLOTTO

BLOTTO

Adventures in Alcoholism
Ruin to Recovery

JEFFREY POHN

Redwood Publishing, LLC

First Printing, 2019

Published by Redwood Publishing, LLC (Ladera Ranch, California)

ISBN 978-1-947341-83-8 (paperback)
ISBN 978-1-947341-84-5 (e-book)

Library of Congress Cataloguing Number: 2019914711

Book Design:
– Cover Design: Bienvenido A. Swinton Jr.
– Interior Design: Ghislain Viau

10 9 8 7 6 5 4 3 2 1

For Lexie, my hero

Table of Contents

PREFACE

A couple of years ago, my bright and extremely inquisitive nephew, Sammy, came to visit during spring break. He had just turned thirteen, the age at which I began my drinking career. One evening, we were hanging out together, watching Chicago Bulls basketball, when Sammy asked me a simple question, "How come you don't drink?" The answer wasn't so simple. In my attempt to respond, I'm not sure if I was delivering a cautionary tale or just trying to entertain my little nephew, but the more I divulged, the more Sammy bombarded me with questions. In a Q&A session lasting over an hour, I got an unexpected kick out of recounting my often dark, occasionally humorous, drinking adventures, many of which I hadn't thought about in years. Sammy seemed to truly enjoy hearing these tales (he even lowered the volume on the TV). In the ensuing days, with these remembrances swirling around in my head, other episodes bubbled up, and soon I had the idea—no, the compulsion—to write them down.

I would like to be able to say that every word of this book is true, but I must admit to some memory damage, having lost quite a few brain cells from the activities written about herein. It is my sincere hope that anyone dealing with alcoholism and/or addiction will relate to my experience, and that it could be helpful in overcoming these kinds of afflictions.

An estimated eighteen million Americans suffer from alcoholism. Sixty-five million binge-drink. In the world, there are approximately two-hundred-forty million alcoholics, and those numbers don't take into account drug addicts, or the countless family members and loved ones affected by their alcoholic/addict.

Currently, in addition to 12-step programs for alcohol and drugs, there are over fifty different programs worldwide, including groups for spenders, clutterers, kleptomaniacs, liars, procrastinators, debtors, online gamers, gang members, etc. Programs exist for people who have devastating obsessions with food, nicotine, gambling, shopping, sex…even feet.

This is my story.

Names have been changed to protect the innocent…and the guilty.

1
BOTTOMS UP

My days are devoted to the killing of cockroaches, who share my scuzzy, single apartment in Hollywood. I'm drinking around the clock, but to diminishing returns. I have to drink more and more to achieve the desired affect—Blotto. I buy my booze at different liquor stores, so that the guys behind the counter don't recognize me as a drunk. My body wakes me up in the middle of night, demanding alcohol. I sleep with a cheap bottle of vodka under my bed, and I am gifted tiny vials of cocaine from a sweetheart of a dealer, who knows I can no longer afford to pay.

A growing paranoia darkens my shrinking world; I sleep with a carrot peeler on the bedside table. Suspecting my phone is bugged, I take it completely apart, forgetting that it was disconnected months ago. Other than liquor runs, I hardly ever leave the apartment, but when I do, I suspect I'm being followed. I don't want anyone to witness what I've become. My only human contact is with the mailman, through the slot. For years, I drank exclusively hi-end booze, like the brands I was weened on, from my parents' liquor cabinets. Now, I'll guzzle anything at all, including, in desperate moments, Paco Rabanne cologne.

I'm not a bad guy—I'm well educated. I love my mother. I floss semi-regularly. So, how did I wind up like this, at thirty-years-old? Allow me take you back to where it all began, as I remember it...

2
LAKESIDE

The soles of a woman's feet, as seen through the eyes of a five-year-old, from inches away. My earliest memory. The soles are covered with tiny, fresh cuts, many still bleeding. I press myself against the foot of a king-sized bed where my mother, Laura, lies on her back with her feet up on a pillow, nursing another Bloody Mary, smoking a Pall Mall, and watching Groucho Marx on TV. A striking twenty-eight-year-old, my mom believes she looks more than a little like the soon-to-be first lady, Jackie Kennedy.

Earlier that autumn day in 1960, one of the last warm ones before the brutal Chicago winter, mom took me to the beach, down the cliff from our home. After a picnic lunch of camembert and crackers, I announce that I have to tinkle. Mom makes a display of annoyance, picks me up, and heads toward the rickety beach house which has been recently vandalized—there are broken windows, and the floor is littered with tiny pieces of glass. She carries me in her arms across the glass shards to the washroom where I can pee properly.

Back home, I can't stop staring at the cuts on the bottoms of my mother's feet, mesmerized by the carnage—an image that becomes seared in my mind. Why couldn't she just let me pee in the sand or in the lake? Why does everything have to be so fancy? Is this my fault?

"Dammit!" cries mom, "I have to go to the bathroom."

"I can carry you," I offer.

Mom chuckles, "Silly rabbit, Duffy, you're way too small."

I know someone who could carry her, easy. He's big and strong…but pretty wobbly.

My father, Bernie, is a bit of a mystery to me; unpredictable, bohemian, kind of a swashbuckler, but distant, not quite real, more like a character in a movie. A writer, and a gifted painter, dad draws and paints with me—it's our primary interaction. A nude painting dad did of mom on their honeymoon, called *I Haven't a Thing to Wear*, is prominently displayed in our home, a somewhat unnerving image to see every morning over Cocoa Puffs.

Everyone says that my dad has the greatest sense of humor, but I don't get most of his jokes. The one where he says, "Why don't Jews drink?" (wait for it…) "Because it dulls the pain!" is especially confusing because dad *is* a Jew and he *does* drink. Mom jokes too, calling her husband "the Tarzan of mood swings."

As far as I can tell, my dad is not like other dads. He seems to have no normal job, and does not like normal sports. Dad's sports are skiing, tennis, and his big passion, sailing. He spends more time on his boat than at home, or work, whatever that is. He's a great sailor with lots of trophies, and a bad driver, with lots of car accidents. And I forgot to mention the other sport he loves, one that not too many dads are into—bullfighting.

Dad travels almost every year to the *Running of the Bulls* in Spain. He brings back gifts for me, like real, sharp bull horns, a red cape, and a colorful, tight-fitting matador's outfit. After he's had a few drinks, he has me put on the matador outfit and stand way down the long hall, holding the cape, in trembling fingers. At the other end of the hall, dad starts snorting and pawing the floor with his feet, and holding the bull horns to his head, he charges maniacally down the hall directly at me, his petrified son. Olé!

3
I LOVE PARIS

Bernie can terrorize his son, but he can't scare his wife. Laura is a tough, strong-minded, outspoken woman, and a world-class paddle ball player. She is in charge of raising me and my little sister, Amy, with a laser focus on manners and culture. Her insistence on perfect manners makes me feel like I spend most of my childhood pulling out chairs for large ladies.

But it goes beyond just manners. Mom tries to instill in her children the idea that everyone, no matter who, be treated with respect. Regarding culture, her mission is to expose her kids to everything, including museums, the opera, the symphony, classic literature, Broadway musicals, and drag queen shows.

Mom's demanding social calendar means that she's out most evenings. On the rare night home, she often gives me a bath. Drying me afterward, she sings the song, "I Love Paris," replacing the word "Paris" with Duffy. Later, when I hear the real song, without my name, I feel tricked; I thought that song was about *me*.

My parents fight all the time. I don't see how they ever got married. Years later, I'm told that when my parents first got together, they were the ideal couple, madly in love and dashingly attractive, both from prominent Chicago families. Then, as pressure mounted on dad, with two children and the need to maintain a lavish lifestyle, he started to drink. Rumors that mom had an affair with her sister's husband didn't help. Now, as I listen to them through the wall at night, it sounds like the professional wrestling on TV. One day, in front of my sister and me, mom screams about divorce while beating dad with her high heel.

My need to escape my parents' ongoing war finds me in one of two demilitarized zones—mom's shoe closet or in front of the TV. Mom is proud of her size six feet and has built a shrine to them in the form of an enormous shoe closet, filled top to bottom with an amazing array of footwear. I spend entire afternoons in her closet, my shelter from the storm.

The TV also provides an oasis for me, in the company of my many cartoon friends; Alvin and the Chipmunks, Clutch Cargo, Tom Terrific, Mr. Peabody and his boy Sherman, Rocky and Bullwinkle, and Garfield Goose. My favorite show is The Flintstones, perhaps because everyone in Bedrock is barefoot.

4
SPLIT

Mom takes Amy and me to the circus, the perfect place to inform us about the imminent divorce. Amy and I are too distracted to really get it. I gaze up with rapt attention at the trapeze artists. When the male flyer falls fifty feet, all eyes follow him to the net below, except mine, which remain fixed on the female flyer's pretty pointed toes.

After the divorce, mom moves us from the suburbs to the city. Our new apartment is worthy of Architectural Digest, but the move is a rough transition for me; I'm grossed out by the dog poop I have to dodge on the walk to school, unnerved at having to take an elevator to our apartment in the company of the ancient, boozy elevator man, and not thrilled to be the "new boy" at a new school.

Education is extremely important to our family; my paternal grandmother, Nonnie, never stops reminding me about the importance of good schooling, "Duffy, you listen to me, you.

Education means money, and money means power, which is what you got to have for when (not if) the Nazis return." Nonnie, the sharp-tongued but much-adored family matriarch, is a real fixture in the lives of her eleven grandchildren…a focal point. We cousins believe that Nonnie has a ranking system for all of us, connected to what promises to be an massive inheritance. For many years, all of her grandchildren jockey for position, currying favor, and sharing information and rumors about who is in the top spot, and who might have fallen in the rankings. When Nonnie passes away, decades later, she leaves behind only a small piggy bank.

Mom enrolls us in the "best" private school in Chicago, a stuffy, preppy, WASP-infested, K through 12 institution, where I have to wear a tie and jacket every day. It's a suffocating place, with windows that don't open, and gray industrial carpeting throughout. I soon discover that I am the only Jewish kid in first grade when a classmate calls me "Christ Killer." A bunch of the kids take up the chant. Oddly, this instills in me a feeling of accomplishment. Later, I find paintings of Jesus in mom's coffee table art books, and I'm horrified by depictions of the crucifixion, especially the spikes driven through the poor guy's feet.

5
FROZEN NORTH

After the divorce, a bachelor again, dad rents a top floor apartment in a lakefront high-rise with a commanding view of his beloved Lake Michigan. His place is filled with sailing trophies, stacks of books, and his half-finished paintings, quite a few depicting naked ladies. I spend a good amount of time looking at his paintings, and I find myself drawn to the smell of the paint.

The custody agreement gives dad his children every weekend, and being with him is fun, at first. Dad is the only person I know who owns a tape recorder. Dad, Amy and me gather around the recorder like it's a campfire. Dad records Hemingway short stories. I do imitations—W.C. Fields and Sammy Davis, Jr. are my best. Amy sings over and over, the song "Where is Love?" from the musical, "Oliver," and dad gets angry at me when I tease her. After promising for years, dad finally takes us to sleep overnight on his sailboat. He cooks alphabet soup for dinner in his tiny galley, but Amy throws up, and I pretend I can read the letters in her puke, "It says 'Amy barfed'." Dad likes my joke. Later, he covers us with sails in our bunks, and actually tucks us in.

I am thrilled to be enjoying weekends with dad, but after a few months, Amy refuses to be with him. She is scared of dad, his explosive rages, his erratic driving, and his drinking, which I rationalize as just a "guy thing." Amy's sense of self-preservation is keener than mine. Although, Amy does run away from dad's in the middle of winter, only to be found, after a desperate search, in the park, sitting on frozen pond.

Amy is a bright, sweet-natured child with an unfortunate collection of childhood curses; she's overweight, has a mouthful of braces, thick eyeglasses…and a pretty crazy brother. Amy claims that her earliest memory is of me, standing outside her crib, holding a lighted match. Mom, who is obsessed with externals and perfection, is hard on Amy. I'm a million times worse than Amy, but I seem to get a pass; nothing I do is frowned upon. I adore Amy, but I'm an angry kid and not really nice to anyone. Amy is around me all the time, and becomes the convenient target of much of my rage.

When I'm not beating up on Amy, I am her protector. If anyone lays a hand on my little sister, the punishment is swift and painful. Once, when a kid named Trevor punched Amy, I forced him to swallow a whole shaker of salt. After Trevor had his stomach pumped out, he never bothered Amy again. She is my confidant and sidekick, and nobody messes with her but me.

Left alone quite a lot, Amy and I invent games and adventures, in which Amy often gets the short end of the stick. One day we create an adventure called North Pole Explorers; even though it's summer, we dress in parkas, gloves and ski masks. Our miniature schnauzer, Willie, is the husky pulling the sled. Amy plays the girl in the cave to be rescued by the explorer, me. The cave is a closet where I pile clothes on top of Amy, so if a bad guy enters the cave, Amy will be hidden.

Just as I begin my trek though the frozen north, the doorbell rings. It's my downstairs neighbor and best friend, Abe. He and I hang out for a few hours, and then I hear mom call that dinner's ready. She says she can't find Amy. I sprint to the closet, and under the clothes, I find Amy, still there, sweating up a storm in her parka, and smiling her always good-natured smile.

"Thank goodness you found me, Explorer. Did you get lost?"

The quick-thinking explorer responds, "No, a polar bear was chasing me, and I had to kill him."

"How did you know he was a him?"

"Explorers can tell."

Amy nods, accepting my explanation, and everything else about her brother.

6

LICENSE TO KILL

Splitting time between my still-at-each-others-throats parents seems to create a kind of split in me. Thinking I have to please and remain loyal to whichever parent I'm with at the time, I develop a chameleon-like ability to behave completely differently around each one. I am able to alter my personality, depending on what the situation requires—a talent I would perfect in later years.

Dad runs a much looser ship than mom; he allows me to watch TV all night long, doesn't make me wear pajamas to bed, isn't upset when I don't flush, and serves chocolate ice cream for dinner, with an occasional cigar after the meal. There's something cool but also disturbing about being with dad, who puts me on his lap in his Karmann Ghia, and lets me drive on the icy streets of Chicago. In summer, dad has me steer his sixty foot sailboat, "Freebooter," where I'm part of a crew with his new girlfriend, Brandi, who is even more wobbly than dad. Hand on the tiller, I peer into the boat's cockpit, and spot dad playing with Brandi's feet, in broad daylight.

Billy Bowen is a college guy who races with dad, on Freebooter. Dad never stops talking about him—"Billy's so smart, Billy's so funny, Billy's such a good sailor." I've never met Billy, but I hate him. I imagine him as a younger version of dad; handsome, with hair on his chest, drinking the beer dad drinks, and even wearing the boat shoes dad wears, Topsiders.

Dad gets moody when he drinks. He veers between belting out songs from the musical, *Camelot* to ranting about the things he hates, like the outrageous harassment of Lenny Bruce at the hands of the police, or his mother-in-law's ugly feet. One of dad's passions is James Bond. He reads all the Bond books to me, and takes me to Bond movies. He even purchases the same gun Bond uses, and shoots it out of his apartment window, into the city below. Then, one day, he hands me the gun. It's pretty heavy. I just look at it.

"Shoot!" dad commands.

I shake my head "no," feeling smaller than I usually do.

"Are you saying "no" to *me*?"

"I guess."

"I'm your father."

"I'm your son."

"You don't have to hit anything, Duffy. Just shoot, see what it feels like."

"Can't we just paint?"

"Not until we do this, first."

"Why do I have to do it?"

"Because I want you to know what it means to be a man."

"I'm *not* a man."

"Alright, I'm taking you home to your mommy's."

"Fine with me."

"That does it. You shoot or you get shot."

I'm pretty sure my dad doesn't really mean it, but with him, I never know. I take the gun, and with my eyes closed tight, I shoot out of the window. It shakes me up pretty bad. Dad takes the gun from my hand.

"Nice shooting, Deadeye. I think you hit a guy crossing the street."

"What?!" I say with alarm.

"Easy, pardner. Just yankin' your lariat."

Dad pulls me close to him, makes me look into his face.

"Duffy, I want you to listen. What we just did is our secret. You can't tell anyone, especially your mom."

For years afterward, I wonder if I did kill anyone.

7
FOOT NOTES

Around this time dad mysteriously disappears, and stops picking me up for our visits, leaving me at mom's for the weekends. Mom has interesting friends—men who act like ladies, ladies who act like men, and some regular ladies like mom—nice people but I can't see myself tossing the football around with any of them.

Blasting perpetually from mom's hi-fi in the living room are Broadway show tunes. I can't avoid listening, and I make the fateful mistake of memorizing the songs from *Fiddler On the Roof*. Mom throws a huge holiday party, before which she turns her eight-year-old son into a eighty-year-old Jewish man, with a long white beard, a long black coat, and a very long face. The last thing in the world I want to do is entertain a mob of sloppy drunk socialites. But, as with so much in my life, I am powerless.

Hidden in the powder room, in full old-Jewish-man costume, I peer through a crack in the door at the party—a room full of noisy guests who look like a bunch of Batman villains. The rented piano player is playing, but I can't hear him over the din. It's late and I'm sleepy. My beard is itching me. The piano player clinks a glass, and introduces me. I don't move. Mom enters the powder room and gently pushes me into the living room. I trudge to the front of the room. I suppress the overwhelming urge to flee, and I begin to sing "If I Were a Rich Man," from *Fiddler*. The guests explode, howling and laughing and pointing at me. I can't remember feeling more horrible. I had no way of knowing that this experience would kick off a lifelong fear of performance (and public speaking). For years afterward, I won't raise my hand in class, even when I know the answer.

I find that I'm shying away from other things, too; mom is a member of a pool club where I've always enjoyed swimming, but suddenly, I refuse to go in the pool. It seems strange that a guy whose dad spends so much time on the water would be afraid of being in the water. Every time I am about to swim, I imagine that if I go underwater, I will surface in the middle of the ocean, surrounded by sharks. Much to mom's chagrin, I just sit poolside, gazing at the parade of feet, especially female feet, stepping in and out of the pool. These images are so engrossing that later at dinner, I feel too full to eat.

At school recess, my pals and I compare notes on our favorite new preoccupation—girls. The guys offer insights and analyses on our female classmates' bosoms, butts, and legs. I comment on a girl's nice-looking feet. The guys look at me like I'm out of my mind. They tease me, and call me names like "Foot Freak" and "Toe Jam Man." It's clear to me that I have yet another secret to keep.

I attempt to understand why I find the female foot so intoxicating. When I see a girl or a woman, I look first at the feet, then make my way up to their face. Most people look at the face first, then move their way down. I simply know that when I focus on feet, I feel better. I am able to escape. I forget myself. I disappear. I can no longer be seen or judged or hurt. I start secretly sketching feet from mom's *Vogue* magazines, and when I wind up at dad's place, the forbidden *Playboys*.

The apartment building where we live, on Chicago's near-north side, is near Hugh Hefner's Playboy mansion. I invite my pal, Abe, to join me on the roof of our fourteen story building, to enjoy a major discovery that I've recently made—the unobstructed view of Hefner's rooftop, where in the summer, Playboy bunnies sunbathe topless. This magnificent spectacle is made even more wondrous with the binoculars I stole from dad. I guess living in the city isn't so bad after all.

8
ETTA IS BETTA

Over time, I see less and less of dad. My home and my life are dominated almost exclusively by females—Mom, Amy, my grandmother, Nonnie, and a couple of aunts. Even our dog, Willoughby, is a bitch. I am particularly close to my aunt Carolyn, dad's sister. She is a wonderfully wacky and warm woman who often invites me to her suburban home for weekends, where I hang out with her four sons, my cousins. At Carolyn's, I'm allowed to get dirty, wear cutoffs, use swear words, and feel like a real boy.

I'm also close to my mother's sister, my Aunt Jody. She lives only a couple blocks away, and whenever I run away from home, I run to Aunt Jody's. She is not nearly as formal as mom, plays tennis with me, and compliments my strokes. Her home is much more relaxed than mine, and she has two sons around my age, Hubie and Johan, with whom I have much in common. We have dirt wars with the neighbor kids, draw pictures of naked ladies, and erase the eyeballs on the covers of fashion magazines.

The closest thing I have to a male role model is actually a female—our elderly, black housekeeper, Etta, who is warm in ways that mom is not, and seems to be more involved in my day-to-day life. Etta takes me to White Sox baseball games on Chicago's south side, and she teaches me the finer points of the game. Etta coaches, encourages, and helps me to become a good little athlete and a big sports fan. I follow Chicago sports teams in the paper, listen to games on the radio, and master an exhaustive array of statistics. Etta has extremely mangled, arthritic feet, and she sometimes asks me to rub lotion on them. Etta's are the only unattractive feet I ever touch, and I'm happy to do so.

I am aware that mom is a big fan of plastic surgery, so I ask her if that kind of thing could help Etta's feet.

"It's sweet of you to think of that, Duffy, but I doubt plastic surgery could help Etta…though it might work wonders on your nose."

"My nose? What's wrong with my nose?"

"Nothing, sweetheart. I was just joking. You have a gorgeous nose."

Maybe mom is just kidding, but I take it very personally, and I run with the comment. It almost seems like I want to create pain for myself. I never thought anything was wrong with my nose, never thought about my nose…period. But, displaying the hypersensitivity that would become a defining trait of mine, I allow mom's minor joke to set off a major campaign of self-inspection, as I now spend hours in front of the mirror, examining my nose, along with my eyes, ears, lips, skin, hair, and everything else.

9

TOGETHERNESS

Television still serves as a much-needed refuge for me. Cartoons have been replaced by live action shows like *Twilight Zone*, *The Man from U.N.C.L.E*, and *Get Smart*. But I am most drawn to shows that depict family life—*My Three Sons*, *Dick Van Dyke*, *Hazel*, and especially the show about the family I'd most like to be a part of, *Leave it to Beaver*. I don't just watch this show, I *enter* it.

I become the older brother, and all-around good kid, Wally, and I also assume the role of Eddie Haskell, Wally's weaselly, wise-ass friend. The Jekyll & Hyde nature of this duel role is a natural for me. For Wally's younger brother, Beaver, I see my sister, Amy. I can't imagine my parents as the parents in the show; The dad, Ward, is always at home, has no bad habits, no craziness, he pretty much just smokes a pipe, and smiles. And the mom, June Cleaver, is what God must have had in mind when he invented mothers. All of the families in these shows are so much different than mine. I wonder what you'd call a show about *my* family—maybe *Father Knows Shit*.

Without notice, dad starts showing up again for our weekends at his place. He seems to be in worse shape than ever. In the car ride to his apartment, dad keeps trying to run over pigeons. That's exactly the kind of thing that made Amy not want to be with him.

"Where you been?" I ask my dad.

"What do you mean?"

"You didn't pick me up for the weekend…a bunch of weekends!"

"I've been out of town. Checking out a new boat in Florida."

"You go alone?"

"Billy Bowen came with."

I feel stung and betrayed.

"You guys homos?"

Dad raps me in the head with his knuckles, then guns for another pigeon.

At dad's apartment, I discover that his girlfriend, Brandi, is living with him now, and his apartment is a pig sty. I don't know which is worse…mom's home where the living room is to look at, not sit in, a place where I'm not allowed to get dirty, or dad's apartment, which is such a mess you can't *help* getting dirty.

That night, I knock on dad's bedroom door to say good-night. His slurry voice instructs me to come in, have a seat. I enter, and sit in a corner chair. Dad and his girlfriend are in bed, both obviously drunk. I then watch in astonishment as my dad and Brandi start to have sex. Ward Cleaver would *never* do anything like this. I think I should leave, but something glues me to the chair. I know that it's wrong for me to be seeing this, and I'm totally freaked out, but at least dad and I are doing something together.

The following morning, dad once again makes me promise not to say anything to anyone. This is the biggest secret yet, and the hardest one to keep.

10

SPIT TAKE

I am one pissed off ten-year-old. I can't control anything in my life, especially how other people behave. Mom is becoming a dating machine. I'm not happy about that. It sounds insane, but I still cling to the dream of my parents getting back together.

When mom's dates arrive, she insists that I greet them at the door, fix them a drink, and "entertain" them until she makes her entrance. Mom decrees that I must look perfect. She spends more time dressing me than herself. Perfect clothes. Perfect hair. I don't know why *I* have to look so good, the dates are interested in my hot mama, not me. These horn-dogs, a collection of combovers, fatsos, phonies, and walking pinkie rings, seem pleased with themselves. So, to take them down a notch, when I mix drinks for the dates, I often spit in them. I get a kick out of watching the dates drink my cocktails. I go out of my way to make the dates uncomfortable, bringing up conversational topics like their ex-wives or the holocaust. Before the dates arrive, I strategically place plastic vomit and dog poop around the living room, and I smile innocently as the dates do double-takes.

The date I dislike the most, Seymour, a man with three kids from a previous marriage, none of whom will speak to him, becomes mom's third husband (there was one before Bernie who I won't even find out about for years). Seymour is outwardly impressive, a tall, handsome architect, with skyscraper drawings on his office wall. But he actually only builds squat, ugly retirement homes.

Seymour moves in with us. He has the ugliest feet I've ever seen. I have zero interest in men's feet, not even my own, but with Seymour now living under my roof, I'm confronted with his disgusting dogs every day. It turns out that my new step-father is a real drinker, a big-time liar, and a bully. At six-foot-four, and well over two-hundred pounds, it's easy for him to get rough with me, and knock me around. I don't understand why Seymour only throws underhand with a football, but overhand when hurling a full glass of scotch at me.

I don't know how my mom could have married this creep. The only thing I can figure is that with Seymour, a male, she can now join a country club, and mom loves country clubs. I'm not a big fan. When Seymour takes us to the club, I have to accompany him to the men's locker room, where, in the steam room, I encounter groaning old men with balls down to the ground. I despise these guys who refer to Seymour as "your dad." I get my revenge by peeing into shampoo bottles, then watching with glee as the club members wash their hair.

11
NATURE BOY

Mom becomes pregnant with twins. I really want at least one boy. But when Jewel and Liza are born, I adore them anyway, from moment one. Mom, and especially Seymour, seem somewhat hands-off with the girls. They are fine with Etta doing most of the heavy lifting, with an assist from Amy and me. I'm fascinated with my new little sisters, and I love being around them, looking at them, playing with them, feeding them. I do draw the line at diaper-changing.

Shortly after the twins are born, Seymour decides that I have to go to summer camp. I am not consulted. Seymour's choice of a camp is bizarre; I am totally obsessed with playing sports, so Seymour determines that the best thing for me is a *nature* camp, where I will learn how to pitch a tent and identify poison ivy.

I arrive at the camp, in northern Minnesota, to discover that it is a hotbed of sadism; the counselors, who I had hoped were the kind of male role models I've never really had, are instead, monsters; the counselors put Ben-Gay in the campers' underpants, which scorches our genitals, and they make us have boxing matches, with the losers forced to sleep outside.

The oldest boy in my cabin, Ronnie, is a serious sicko, with a penchant for torturing the younger kids. One day, Ronnie is giving a little kid a "Pink Belly," where he slaps the kid's stomach until it's red and sore. The kid escapes, and dashes toward the cabin door. Ronnie yells for him to halt. When the kid keeps running, Ronnie grabs a dart from a dartboard, sprints to the doorway, and hurls the dart, which hits the kid's leg, and downs him like a deer.

I become scared that Ronnie is going to target me next, so I become his henchman. On a canoe trip, while our counselor is napping in his tent, Ronnie takes me and a chubby kid named Pauly on a hike into the woods. Ronnie instructs me to tie Pauly to a tree, and we smear honey on Pauly's face. Ronnie tells Pauly there's a man-eating bear in the woods, then Ronnie and I hide, and watch Pauly freak out. After a couple of hours, we untie Pauly, and Ronnie warns him if he ever rats on us, he's a deadman. It's like a Jewish *Lord of the Flies*, and I'm decidedly *not* one of the good kids. What I'm doing is awful, and I know it, but I have to admit it feels liberating. Finally, I have an outlet for my intense anger, one that also gives me a rare feeling of power.

The single worst thing about summer camp, even worse than the sadism, is that we are made to write letters home each week to our parents. Unlike any of the other campers, I have to write *two* letters, one to mom, and one to dad. Not a single other boy's parents are divorced. We have to write these letters sitting close together around a table. For me, this is torture. My parents' divorce is a source of burning shame and embarrassment. I never speak about it. I don't want any of the boys at camp to know. I worry that having divorced parents will make me look weak, and therefore, a more vulnerable target for the bullies. Little did I know, that in a few years, most of my friend's parents would be getting divorced.

12
OVER MY SKIIS

Dad invites me to go on a ski trip with him to Vail, Colorado. Mom is worried about dad's state of mind, and tells me I don't have to go. But I'm still holding on to my crazy hope that dad and I could have some kind of real relationship. On the plane to Colorado, I sit next to dad.

"Dad, could you hand me that magazine."

"Good to hear you call me dad."

"Well, that's your title."

"What do you call Seymour?" dad asks.

"Asshole," I answer.

"Your mother has terrible taste in men."

A stewardess wheels a drink cart to our seats.

"Can I get you gentlemen anything to drink?"

"Scotch for me, couple of those little bottles," dad orders.

"Make it three," I casually say to the stewardess.

"No!" dad says, almost angrily.

"Oh, it's okay for you to drink all the time, but I can't even have a little taste?"

"When you're my age you can drink as much as you want…I just hope you don't *need* to."

Dad is quite a good skier, and I'm not too bad myself. I've been looking forward to us conquering the slopes together, but on our first day at Vail, dad says he's feeling too sick to ski. What he means is, too drunk to ski. I can't believe it, although it was entirely predictable. I go off miserably, to ski alone. The ski lift drops me off at the top of the mountain, and I promptly collapse on my skis. I can't do it. I'm paralyzed. I've been skiing all my life, and suddenly, I just can't do it. I don't know what's happening to me. I inch down the hill on my butt. It takes forever, but I finally make it down to the base of the mountain, tears frozen on my cheeks. I can't imagine this trip can get any worse, but it does. The next day, dad finds out that his young sailing buddy, Billy Bowen has been killed in a car accident. Dad is inconsolable.

Dad hasn't been out of the hotel room since we got here, so I convince him to go out for dinner to a restaurant, where he'll have to pay attention to me, across the table. At the restaurant, dad is despondent, he can't stop blubbering about Billy Bowen. I've never seen my dad crying, but he is now. It's clear that he loves Billy. What does Billy have that I don't have? It's like I'm not even there. Finally, I just explode. I start saying to dad, over and over, "I killed Billy Bowen, I killed Billy Bowen." Dad looks at me with the most hateful expression I've ever seen. He grabs a huge bowl of strawberries from a nearby waitress, and dumps the contents over my head. It's so shocking I almost lose consciousness. People at the restaurant become hushed, they stare at us. I hope the color of the strawberries camouflages how bright red my face has become.

The ski trip is over, two days in, but we can't get a refund on our plane tickets. For the next couple of days in our hotel room, dad says almost nothing, he just drinks and draws. Amazingly, his drawings are still excellent. Without anything else to occupy my time, I do some artwork, too—lots of faceless skiers, impaled with ski poles. White snow, red blood. A nice contrast.

1 3
ARTIST IN RESIDENCE

The artistic ability I seem to have inherited from my dad is put to good use at school where I sit in the back of class, entertaining my pals with lovingly rendered, pornographic drawings of our teachers. One day, a jerk named Skip, rips a drawing I'm working on from my notebook, and he runs it up to our English teacher, Mr. Mitchell, who peers at the drawing, then asks, sternly, "Who drew this?" Skip identifies me. Mr Mitchell glares at me, says, "See me after class, Rembrandt."

After everyone has filed out of class, I cower in the front row, sweating bullets as my teacher gazes at the drawing for what feels like hours. My drawing depicts Mr. Mitchell with an enormous penis, having sex with one of his female students. Finally, Mr. Mitchell looks up from the drawing, and says to me, "I must say, this is really quite good." I always liked Mr. Mitchell.

Mr. Mitchell also coaches our school football team, and I am the quarterback. Being QB of the football team means everything to me. It means girls pay attention to me, boys kiss my ass, and I can get away with more shit than ever. It means middle-school stardom. The football field is the happiest place on earth.

The only drawback is that my dad attends the games while visibly drunk. On the sidelines, he argues with other parents, falls down, and makes more than one appalling scene. This is profoundly embarrassing to me. I tell dad he doesn't really need to attend games, but he insists. I can't figure out how a guy who pretty much ignored me my whole life now never misses my football games. After struggling mightily with this dilemma, I finally make the incredibly painful decision that I have to quit the team. It's beyond crushing for me to do this, but I just can't bear the ugly scenes dad makes in front of the kids at school. I tell Coach Mitchell that I injured my foot badly, and can no longer be on the team. Mitchell is skeptical, he figures it has something to do with my dad. Still, the coach seems pissed at me; any coach hates losing his QB. In the end, I say goodbye to my only claim to fame, one of my few adult allies, and to add insult to injury, I have to fake a limp at school for the rest of the year.

Mom and Seymour are out for the evening, as usual. Skip is sleeping over because he is the son of a friend of mom's. Skip has replaced me as the football team's quarterback since I had to hang up my spikes. Skip seems a little too proud of himself. Our housekeeper Etta loves me like a son, but I'm so misbehaved that Etta has been threatening for years to beat me with her weapon of choice, a hard rubber slipper. The combination of her arthritis and my young legs makes that virtually impossible. The night Skip sleeps over, I have him sleep in my own bed, while I sleep in the one across the room.

At bedtime, I turn out all the lights in my room. I even unscrew bulbs, then I start to yell insults at Etta. She yells back at me a few times from the kitchen, and finally charges into my dark bedroom, makes a beeline for my bed, and thinking it's me, Etta starts to beat the daylights out of Skip with her slipper. Skip is no match for Etta. A quarterback has to be tougher than that. I almost smother myself trying to drown my laughter in a pillow.

14
MANHOOD

Completely out of the blue, Seymour announces at dinner that he has spoken with his rabbi, and that I will be bar mitzvah in a couple of months. I desperately do not want to do this, for many reasons: it would have zero meaning for me, I'm terrified of public speaking, I can't possibly learn Hebrew in such a short time, and I would be exposed as a complete and utter fraud. I isolate mom in her marble bathroom, where she removes her make-up, and I appeal to her for mercy.

"You gotta get me outta this, mom. I can't do it."

"Come on, Duffy, not all Jewish boys are lucky enough to afford a bar mitzvah."

"Since when are we such big-time Jews?"

"This means so much to Seymour."

"Then let Seymour make a fool of himself in front of a million brainwashed idiots."

"Where does all this anger come from?"

"It comes from Seymour!"

"He's trying very hard. You think it's easy to be a step-father to someone like you."

"What's happened to you, mom? You used to be so tough. Now you're just a wet noodle. A puppet."

"Watch your mouth, young man."

"Just cause I let him live here, doesn't mean he can wreck my life."

"Who the hell do you think you are?"

"A fucking human sacrifice is who I am!"

Mom just laughs at me, and motions me out of her bathroom. I am beyond upset and feel betrayed. But there's nothing I can do. The best protest I can muster is to eat all the raw bacon in the fridge.

I have to attend a one-on-one meeting with the rabbi to discuss the upcoming "big day." I plan to plead with the rabbi to call off this farce, but once I enter the rabbi's office, I find myself spooked into silence. The office is uncommonly dark, with an overhead light shining down on the old man's blazing, dyed red hair. The rabbi has a glass eye, and I can't figure out which eye is looking at me. The rabbi's dead wives seem to peer down on me from yellowed photos hanging on the walls. The rabbi refers to Seymour as "your father," calls him "a great man, a great friend to the synagogue." I take in this horror show, thinking, "Screw the synagogue, how 'bout being a great friend to *me*."

On the day I am to become a man, I feel more like a mouse, or a rat, a phony rat. With no time to learn Hebrew, I had to memorize the phonetic Hebrew I will now pretend to read from the holy Torah. Miserable in a three-piece monkey suit and too-short haircut, I slump in a huge, throne-like chair at the front of the cavernous room, which is called—I kid you not—The Frankenstein Center. The room is filled with worshippers, including relatives I've never met, my entire class from school, and my dad, who weaves around, noticeably drunk. Prompted by the rabbi, I shuffle to the podium, and overwhelmed with fear and shame, I begin to perform. In the middle of my Torah portion, I make a mistake. A collective "Oy!" issues from elders in the front row. I stop dead. I've been found out. Everyone knows I'm a fraud. An endless, uncomfortable silence, then I start to cry, and I wet my pants. The boy did not become a man.

Following the bar mitzvah, a fancy luncheon is held in my honor, as though nothing strange has just happened. I can't take it anymore, my head is about to explode. I steal a bottle of vodka from the open bar, and dash into the men's washroom, where I duck into a stall, lock the door, and pull my feet up so no one knows I'm there. I suck on the vodka bottle—my very first drink—and soon a warmth and wonderfulness spreads throughout my being. What an amazing feeling. But it's more like a *lack* of feeling, the best non-feeling I've ever had. Later, I puke my guts out. I can't wait to drink again.

When I finally stumble home, I'm greeted by my furious and humiliated family. Mom calls me, "The worst bar mitzvah boy in history of bar mitzvah boys." I comment, "That's a shitload of boys, especially when you figure Jesus was one of 'em." Seymour slaps me in the face. They all hate me, I have committed the ultimate sin—I made them look bad. But I don't care, I don't feel a thing. Nothing matters. For the first time ever, thanks to my new friend alcohol, nothing matters. Thank fucking God.

15
SAIL AWAY

A few months later, I come home from school to find mom sobbing in a bubble bath. She informs me that my dad has died. Dead at forty-three. I have no reaction. Dad's death is as mysterious as his life. My sister Amy and I are not told anything of the circumstances, only that it had something to do with drinking. I feel guilty that I feel nothing. If anything, there's almost a sense of relief that there is no longer anyone to keep secrets for.

At dad's funeral, mom has me sit in the back of the room with her and Amy. I see my aunt Carolyn usher my grandmother, Nonnie, into the room. Nonnie is extremely unsteady and crazed with grief over the sudden loss of her son. I rush over to them and give them both a hug. Nonnie stares at me like she doesn't recognize me. "He looks just like my Bernie," Nonnie says.

"That's Bernie's *son*, mother, your grandson, Duffy," Carolyn clarifies.

"It's *him*, it's my Bernie!" Nonnie cries out.

Carolyn makes the circling "crazy" sign with her finger, and motions for me to go back to where my mom and sister are sitting.

Dad's older brother, Fat Mac, a reputed member of the Jewish Mafia, and someone who has hardly ever uttered a word to me, approaches. He envelopes me in a bear hug. I discreetly pat him down. No firearms. Fat Mac tells me, "Your father loved you." "Right," I respond. As the rabbi eulogizes dad, talking about someone I barely recognize, all around me, people are weeping. I am not.

A couple of weeks after dad's death, mom notices that I've been moping around the house. She assumes I'm depressed. I'm not really, but I *have* been drinking, every day. She takes me to a movie to cheer me up, but not just any movie, Stanley Kubrick's *Lolita*. The opening credits appear. I gasp. Completely covering the movie screen is a gigantic close-up of an exquisite female foot, with a man's hand painting the toenails. I'm overwhelmed. The shot goes on and on. I feel a powerful stirring in my blue jeans. Moments later, I experience my first orgasm, inches away from my mother.

16
NECTAR OF THE GODS

Before my discovery of alcohol, sounds were always too loud, colors too bright, and feelings too intense. Now, with the magic elixir, everything mellows out. It's similar to the effect female feet have on me, but in hyper-drive. If focusing on feet helped to soften life's blows, booze provides a kind of force field that insulates and protects me from the blows. My fears and worries are dulled, my hyperactive mind is quieted. I can talk to girls. I am able to stop obsessing about my life for brief periods of time. I no longer care what people think about me. I can disappear, and escape from all the things that cause emotional pain...except dad's secret about having sex in front me. That one sticks with me, and keeps me up at night.

Finally, I just can't hold it in any longer. I decide to tell dad's secret to my mom. When I do, she doesn't believe me, and sends me to her shrink. I am terribly uncomfortable betraying my dad, and now to a stranger, but I just can't live with it anymore. First, I'm haunted by the secret, now I'm haunted by the telling of the secret.

Mom's shrink, with the classic name, Dr. Helmut Baum, is a notorious-looking, chain-smoking German, one eye heavily-lidded, his face barely visible behind a cloud of cigarette smoke. It's like I've walked into Lee Marvin's Nazis movie, "The Dirty Dozen," which happened to be the last movie dad ever took me to. I painfully divulge my secret about dad once again, but the shrink doesn't believe me either. He says he wants me to come to his office a few times a week. Nein, Herr Doktor.

When I return home, mom asks how I liked Dr. Baum. I reply, "Not a bad guy, for a war criminal." This sets off a skirmish, but nothing compared to my battles with Seymour, who is constantly cheerleading for the Viet Nam war, and insisting that I am going to enlist when the time comes. Nein, Herr Asshole.

The only thing I like about home is my sisters. The twin girls, Jewel and Liza, are becoming real people; they love riding on my shoulders as we stroll through the neighborhood, and they beg me to read to them at bedtime, often from the R. Crumb comics Liza has pilfered from my bedroom. Jewel is very much like Amy; sweet, gentle, non-confrontational, while Liza is more like me; angry, rebellious, a little nuts.

Case in point; one evening, when mom and Seymour are out, and I'm supposed to be babysitting, Jewel runs into my room, screaming, "Liza is killing Mr. Rogers!" I have no idea who or what Jewel is referring to, but I rush into the twins' room to find Liza standing in front of their fish bowl with a maniacal expression on her face, and the orange head of a live fish poking out of her fist. I take it this is Mr. Rogers. In her other hand, Liza holds a spray bottle of cleanser, which she points threateningly at the fish's head. Jewel is hysterical as I beg Liza not to kill Mr. Rogers. But Liza sprays Mr. Rogers, and drops him into the fish bowl, where he sinks to the bottom. Jewel sobs uncontrollably in my arms. I yell at Liza, demanding to know why she killed Mr. Rogers. She responds by sobbing too, and jumps into my arms for comfort. What Liza did was awful, but I think I understand the kind of anger and lunacy that drove her to it. I hug my little sisters. I feel for them both.

17
I FEEL FREE

My seventeen-year-old cousin Buzz, three years older than me, is a long-haired, ex-jock, who provides my first real exposure to the "counter-culture." Buzz's basement might as well be another planet: black-light posters glowing on the walls, incense burning, one guy in the corner who just rolls joints, and doesn't speak, hippie girls in cut-offs with deliciously dirty, bare feet, and mind-bending music I've never heard, pouring forth from gigantic speakers—Cream, Hendrix, Zappa, The Kinks, Van Morrison, Jethro Tull, The Zombies. I smoke weed for the first time. It has no effect on me at all, but I act like I think a stoned person would. I pretend to see "trails." I walk into walls. No one pays any attention to me. It's like nobody can see me, like I don't exist. I love it. I feel like my favorite R. Crumb character, Fritz the Cat, who becomes invisible, sneaks into the girls' shower, and pops a boner no one can see.

As much as I dig the new sounds in Buzz's basement, I soon find myself drawn to the jazz music I hear emanating from

Etta's radio, and later, the cool, hard-drinking and drugging musicians who inhabit that world. I talk mom into letting me take saxophone lessons. I rent a sax, but I'm not good enough fast enough, so without informing mom, I stop going to the lessons. But, I do have mom continue to rent the sax, which I pretend to play, in the mirror, wearing dark glasses and a beret, and "accompanied" by my favorite Jazz saxophonists, John Coltrane and Charlie Parker. These jam sessions are liberating, and allow me to feel cool. But after a few weeks, mom finds out I haven't been going to the music lessons. She returns the sax, and I return to Rock and Roll.

18
DIRTY HIPPIE

I always had a thing for women's shoes; high heels, espadrilles, flats, sandals, whatever, with a preference for footwear that exposes the most foot flesh. But I'm also into men's shoes, exclusively gym shoes. I have discerning, expensive tastes. I visit sporting goods stores the way one would visit a museum, seriously studying and appraising shoes for hours. I handle them, admire them, but I can't afford to purchase them.

My basketball coach at school, a crewcut ex-marine, has some kind of shoe deal, and he insists that everyone on the team wear the shoes he represents. The coach's shoes are incredibly unattractive and cheaply made, and I refuse to wear them. After a bitter confrontation with the coach, he boots me off the team. But it's really no big deal. The banishment only hastens my transition from "Nice Jewish Boy" to "Dirty Hippie."

I counter Seymour's incessant barking at me to get a haircut by growing my hair past my shoulders. My hair is thick and curly, and I worry that I look like a Jewish Bozo the Clown. I buy the cheapest hair-straightening product I can find, which stinks for days, and makes me vaguely resemble James Taylor on the cover of his new album. I never understood it, but long-haired guys (even gross ones) seem to get the girls, and with my new and noxious locks, I get one too.

Fifteen-year-old Melody is making her own transition, from cheerleader to hippie chick. A blonde-haired, blue-eyed shiksa goddess-in-waiting, Melody is pretty and sweet and innocent—the perfect girlfriend, if not for her Flintstone feet, more Fred than Wilma.

I extend to Abe, an invitation to watch Melody and me making out. I rip off a couple bottles of mom's pricey wine, roll a few joints, drop the needle on 'Layla' by Derek and the Dominoes, and voila, the mood for love. As Melody and I make out, I keep one eye on Abe's reaction—Abe digs it. Melody, not so much.

One of my best pals, Marty, more than anything, loves to be naked. He wants everyone else to be naked, too. Marty achieves this in an ingenious way; he throws a party at his parents' sumptuous home, invites his three or four closest friends for eight o'clock in the evening, and when Marty opens the front door, he's totally nude. Marty so owns his nakedness that it makes others feel awkward and self-conscious being clothed. So, we remove our clothes, and when the next wave of guests arrive at eight thirty, they are badly outnumbered by naked people, and they too, disrobe.

And on it goes, every half hour, a new wave of guests arrive, most of whom wind up feeling the obligation to be naked. Marty has raided his parents' liquor cabinets, and complemented that with an impressive assortment of drugs. It's an entertaining evening, but the thing that keeps this party from being the kind of orgy that Marty had in mind is that there is a male/female ratio of more than fifteen to one. Marty is a great host, but he was never that good at math.

19
SUCH A DEAL

Using my dad, Bernie, as a negative role model, Laura (as I now call mom) has always tried to impress upon me the importance of being a good businessman. Taking her advice to heart, I start to deal marijuana. The profits from this endeavor, along with the money I swipe from Laura's purse, allow me to afford all the new gym shoes I want. I become known and envied at school for my gym shoe collection.

I am fashioning a new identity—sort of a *very* poor man's Hugh Hefner. In addition to my ever-growing mane and groovy new threads, my bedroom features a waterbed, exotic-looking textiles adorning the walls, a high-end sound system, and my old posters of Chicago sports luminaries replaced by rock stars and pin-ups. Laura doesn't seem to wonder how I'm financing all of this. Socially, I'm moving and shaking, dumping my old friends, and making new ones—older guys, bad apple seniors who are drawn to me because I'm such a cool dude, and for my cheap—and often free—pot.

During my first couple years of high school, my illegal substance activities expand along with my mind. In addition to daily drinking and pot smoking, I experiment freely with LSD, mescaline, cocaine, speed, hashish, Quaaludes, etc. Quaaludes are my favorite, as they get me closest to unconsciousness while still remaining conscious. My least favorite drug is LSD. On my last and worst acid trip, hanging out with a bunch of friends at the home of one of their parents, I sit on the floor with my weight back on my hands. When the others leave to party elsewhere, I become convinced that my hands are glued to the floor. I simply cannot move. I remain stuck there for hours until my friend's parents return home, and find me alone, still hopelessly attached to the floor.

"What are you *doing* here?" the surprised mom demands.

I try to speak, but words won't come out. The best I can do is to nod or shake my head. The dad glares accusingly at me, snaps at his wife.

"Look at his eyes, Doris. He's all hopped up." He trains his disgust on me.

"What the hell's wrong with you?"

I shrug.

"We'd like you to leave," the mom insists.

"Can't," is the best I can manage to say.

I wriggle around on the floor. Finally, the parents get down on their hands and knees, pry me off floor, and send me on my way.

20
THE GHOST OF FAT MAC

Dad's older brother, Fat Mac, passes away from complications related to the flesh eating disease. We don't attend his funeral. A few weeks later, large boxes arrive for me and Amy. Mac had been "holding onto" them for us. In the boxes are many of our dad's possessions; books, clothes, paintings, bullfighter gear, sailing trophies…and a collection of super-8 films. I get hold of a projector, and view the films; every single one is dedicated to me playing football. The shaky camera is trained exclusively on my every move, follows me everywhere, often zooms to a close-up of me in my helmet. I am stunned. It's a confusing, emotional gut punch. I never thought my dad was really all that interested in me, and now…I don't really know how to handle this new revelation, so I resort to my solution to everything; just get and stay high…every waking hour of the day.

I begin to find myself avoiding social interaction, especially eye contact. I start wearing sunglasses indoors. I become convinced that everybody at school is looking at me and talking about me. Easily startled, I overreact to every sound. I become preoccupied with death. My newspaper reading becomes redirected from the sports page to the obituaries. I'm tortured by insomnia. Alarmed by all this, I stop getting wasted for brief stretches, but that only makes things worse, so I dive back in. Destination, Blotto.

I start to skip school, spending my days at a local cinema art house, where I can hide alone in the dark, always with a stash of drugs, booze, and popcorn. I lose myself in the movies, watching my favorites over and over again; *Dr. Strangelove, Rosemary's Baby, Sunset Blvd, Psycho, Repulsion, Touch of Evil.* I note which actresses have the best feet—Brigitte Bardot, Jane Fonda, Elizabeth Taylor. Becoming a film buff helps to slowly morph me from a participant in life into a spectator, and enhances the growing voyeuristic quality of my life. Watching the movie *To Kill a Mockingbird*, I start to sob, overcome with the longing to join Atticus, Jem and Scout in their simpler, black and white world.

2 1
BETTER FIT

I embark on a brief career as a master thief…one who always gets caught. I steal bellbottoms, record albums, rolling papers, booze, and a corned beef sandwich. Mom is mortified, she doesn't want anyone else to know about her wayward son. I am not deterred, and with assistance from my buddy Abe, we begin devising a semi-serious plan to kill my step-father, Seymour. The scheme is dashed when Etta discovers my notebook full of plans and drawings for Seymour's elimination, and she shows them to mom. Around that time, I am suspended from school for the crime of wearing gym shoes, and though it's never mentioned, I'm pretty sure my porn drawings of the teachers have surfaced.

My school is extremely conservative, and insanely competitive. The school posts lists of the impressive colleges their students get into. I think they fear that my college, if I get into one, won't be so impressive. Mom, Seymour and my headmaster arrive at the determination that a different school might be a "better fit" for me, and they send me packing, to a boarding school in Arizona for my final two years of high school.

Set in the Red Rock country, my new school couldn't be more different from my old one; it is incredibly picturesque, permissive, and "progressive," with no dress code. In fact, at a nearby creek, I discover students and teachers hanging out together, totally naked. It's awesome but also disorienting. An educational culture shock. I don't feel all that comfortable here. I get the sense that the other students see me as some sort of rich kid, city slicker. I'm a poor student, but I thrive on the soccer and basketball teams, and I especially enjoy the coed, after-dinner volleyball games. It's the only time I interact with females. For some reason, I won't go near the girls' dorm.

I take full advantage of the fact that alcohol and drugs are readily available at this school. My frequent cocaine use produces a paranoia in me, and I become suspicious that the administration is suspicious of me. I get a friend of mine, Jamie, to hide my booze in his room. Jamie is caught with my bottles, and is expelled from school. Jamie doesn't squeal, and I don't say a word. A while later, I'm caught with alcohol on my breath, and I'm sent before a teacher/student disciplinary committee. I am being judged by the same kids I drink and get high with. Am I going to get kicked out of yet another school? In the end, I am sentenced to a punishment of digging ditches (in front of everyone). It's not the worst thing in the world, but I feel like I'm on death row.

One day, a beautiful girl, Ana, visits me in the ditch. I've seen her from afar, but we've never spoken. She hands me a cup of water, smiles, then walks away. I watch her flexing her high-arched feet after dance class. I am awkward in my attempts to let Ana know that I'm interested in her. I don't know if she's getting the message. I could not feel more lonely, and I desperately want to be with her. Then, late one night, I'm awakened by a soft knocking on my dorm room door. Groggy from yet another night of heavy drinking, I mumble, "C'mon in." The door opens and it's Ana. She enters, smiling sweetly, an absolute vision. Is she real? Ana peers closely at me in the darkness, then a horrified expression appears on her face, and she rushes away. I'm bewildered, until I realize that I am covered in my own vomit.

22

TEENAGE ZOMBIE

Back home for the summer, my insomnia returns in full force. When I am able to sleep, dreams give way to nightmares, featuring disturbing movie fragments, images of violence, and visions of mangled and butchered feet. At a party celebrating the end of my old school's junior year, I am caught drunkenly trying to cut off the tip of the too-long second toe of a female classmate. I was only joking, but witnesses aren't so sure.

In the middle of a balmy summer night, again I can't sleep, so I borrow Laura and Seymour's precious, vintage Mercedes Benz, and I go on a joy ride. It's a pleasant cruise, until I side-swipe six parked cars. I then, matter-of-factly drive home, park the car in the garage, and go to bed. I am awakened in the morning by my irate step-father

"What the hell did you do?!" Seymour hollers.

"Don't know what you're talking about." I place a pillow over my head.

"You destroyed my car." Seymour rips the pillow off my head.

"*Your* car? It's mom's car. She paid for it."

"Get your worthless ass out of bed."

"Get *your* worthless ass out of my room."

Seymour hauls me out of bed, and starts throwing me around the room. The rest of the family gather at the door, terrified. Seymour slaps me in the face, hard. In response, and fueled by years of pent up fury, I haul back and punch Seymour in the jaw. A real haymaker. The big man crumples to the floor. It's the first and only time I have ever punched anyone in the face. I briefly survey the damage, and walk out of the room as if nothing happened.

Finally, Laura and Seymour become aware that something is seriously wrong with me. They lock up the liquor cabinets and search my room, but they don't have to monitor my comings and goings; I remain holed up in my bedroom, only leaving the house to restock my supply of liquor, which I purchase with a fake ID. I know the family is watching me like hawks whenever I return home, so I wear baggy pants, and tape the little, curved, pint bottles to the inside of my thighs.

Soon, I stop leaving the house at all, and I eat almost nothing. I have no interest in anything, no desire, no energy. I go from being plagued with insomnia to sleeping constantly. Then, one day, I stop talking entirely. I have become a teenage zombie.

I exit the bathroom after my bi-monthly shower, to find Laura and Seymour sitting on my bed. They are staring at my open nightstand drawer, inside of which is a collection of pills I've stolen from Laura's medicine cabinet (sleeping pills, anti-anxiety medication, muscle relaxants). Barely containing their rage and worry, Laura and Seymour grill me about the theft. I respond without affect, I just shrug in answer to all questions, including "Were you planning to kill yourself?" The decision is made on the spot to commit me to a mental hospital. I have no reaction. In contrast, Laura completely flips out, becomes hysterical, looks like she needs to be hospitalized herself.

23
IN THE BIN

Upon my admittance to the loony bin, I'm briefly examined, then heavily medicated. When I come to, in my hospital room, I find, inches away from my face, another face; sweaty and fleshy, a thoroughly chewed cigar stub sticking out of his mouth. This is my roommate, Eugene, who, without introduction, asks me to be his vice-presidential running mate in the upcoming election. I shrug. Eugene takes that as a commitment.

On election night, all twenty-eight patients on the mental ward gather to watch the election returns. At some point, it hits Eugene that he's not going to win, he will be soundly beaten by Richard Nixon. Eugene lifts his bloated body off the couch, and shuffles silently out of the TV room. Moments later, a deafening sound is heard. Eugene is found sitting in his (and my) bathroom sink, which crashed to the floor when he sat in it. Eugene is weeping, and threatens to eat anyone who comes near him.

I am given a private room, a real perk in a place like this, but not enough to prevent an act of desperation. One night, I step up onto a spindly chair, then I tie my belt, dangling from the ceiling, around my neck. The chair teeters. The belt tightens. I prepare to kick the chair away, when a vivid image enters my mind—my mother's face, and how beside herself she would be if I was found with poop in my pants. The thought is simply unbearable. I give myself a raincheck, and come down from the precarious perch.

I continue a life of semi-nonexistence; eighteen hours a day of sleep, some mandatory arts and crafts, and hospital food. The only person I'm allowed phone contact with is my sister, Amy. Our phone calls go something like this;

"Hey, how you doin, Bubba?" Amy asks, trying to sound chipper.

I grunt in response.

"How's the food there?"

"Lotta bologna."

"You love bologna."

I grunt.

"You need anything, books or comics, or anything?"

"Nah."

"How 'bout some nice, warm socks, that kind you like, with the colored toes?"

"You know my gym shoes?" I ask Amy.

Amy is encouraged at an actual sentence from me.

"Course I do."

"You can have 'em."

"But they're yours."

"I won't be needing 'em."

Amy's voice catches, "Why won't you be needing 'em?"

"Just won't," I mumble.

A long silence, Amy starts breaking down.

"I gotta go...dinner."

"Etta cooking?" I ask.

"Meatloaf. She misses you. I do, too. Bye." Click.

A daily shot of her brother's darkness is a real burden for a fourteen-year-old.

Finally, after weeks of monitoring, the institution's head shrink comes up with a diagnosis for me: "Temporary Loss of Self." Not exactly actionable intelligence. I don't *find* myself again until four months later, when I wake up one morning in the bin, in a totally manic state. It's better than the best cocaine. I can't stop talking, thinking, moving, doing. Working at a furious pace, I create artwork; I paint, make prints, and try to sketch the feet of women on the unit. It's hard to find an attractive foot to draw, but at least nobody's going anywhere.

Unable to control my impulses, I steal a wheelchair from an old psychotic patient, and I rampage crazily on wheels through the unit, threatening everyone with a broken plastic soda bottle. My libido returns in full force. I hit on patients, nurses and social workers. I manage to have sex with a woman on the unit, an older (twenty-five) schizophrenic who can tie a shoe with her toes.

I wind up missing my entire senior year in high school, but I do have to attend daily classes in the loony bin, where I am the star pupil, mostly because my fellow "students" are drugged and drooling. Amazingly, I graduate, and am given a diploma, from "Spaulding School for the Handicapped."

I am also given a lithium prescription for manic depression, which I refuse to take consistently, as it makes me feel too stable. And after almost eight months in captivity, I am released back into the world.

24
HIGHER EDUCATION

After being cautioned every single day by shrinks and nurses at the mental hospital, that I am someone who *cannot* drink alcohol or take drugs, on my first day out of the bin, I get as high as I possibly can. I set my sights on college. I want to get the hell out of town, as far away as possible, to a halfway decent school. I discover that this might not be so easy, with my transcripts revealing my graduation from Spaulding School for the Handicapped. Against my mother's wishes, I bypass a college counselor, put a pin in California (where female feet are most widely on display), and I am actually accepted at a small, arty college in northern California.

I plan to drive cross-country to college, with my maternal cousins Johan and Hubie (who will be attending the same school), in a car my grandmother, Nonnie, has promised to buy for me. My pal Abe has thoughtfully made cassette tapes for my journey, containing all kinds of music, with his own off-color labels attached.

I have a couple of Abe's tapes with me when Nonnie and I take a cab to the car dealer. Nonnie is an extremely shrewd negotiator, and I wind up with a steal—a bottom-of-the line, yellow Toyota station wagon for "almost nothing." I thank Nonnie profusely, and give her a big hug. The salesman asks me if I know how to drive stick shift. "Sure," I say. The truth is I've never driven stick, and it shows as I try to negotiate the freeway, with my hysterical grandmother riding shotgun. I try to calm Nonnie down by popping in a cassette of soothing Brazilian music. It works. Nonnie relaxes a little, enjoys the music.

"This is pleasant music. Not like that nonsense I hear your cousins listening to."

"They're uncouth," I say, hoping to knock them down the ladder a few notches.

What is this music called?" Nonnie asks.

"Not sure, Non, it's on the label."

Nonnie gets out her pince nez reading glasses, and reads out loud the label on the cassette.

"Bossa Nova Sucka Dicka?"

I explode in laughter. I don't think I've ever heard anything funnier than my grandmother uttering the words, "sucka dicka."

Once at college, I'm confronted with big decisions: Do I keep my roommate or get rid of him? Which bed am I going to take? Where can I get a mini-fridge for beer, wine, and vodka? And then there's education—ignoring mom's (I'm calling her mom again) insistence that I become a lawyer or a doctor, or perhaps *because* of it, I make the impulsive choice to major in Modern Dance.

I assume my athletic skills will translate to dance. They don't. My usual hungover state makes it even worse, not to mention the dance belt I have to wear under my tights, which crushes the life out of my genitals. To top it off, the women in the dance classes assume I'm gay. But it's all worth it; to be surrounded everyday by talented toes and gorgeous, high-arched feet—at least they look that way from across the room. Everything's better from a distance.

Whatever shame I used to feel about my interest in feet, it's long gone now. In fact, I fancy myself a connoisseur, with a clear notion of the essentials—the ideal female foot shall meet the following standards:

An even and smooth diagonal gradation from big toe to baby toe.

The fourth toe can be somewhat curved but not too curly like a cashew.

The baby toe should not ride up on the fourth toe.

The length of the second toe must not exceed the big toe, by too much.

A fleshy big toe is preferred.

Toenails have to be well-manicured, never jagged or too long—nothing is a bigger turn-off than talons.

Painted toenails are fine, but best to stay away from dark blue and black, which tend to make the toes look too pale.

Toe rings are acceptable, if not too prominent.

What is *not* acceptable are bunions, corns, and hammer toes.

Last but certainly not least, no female foot should be without a glorious high arch, which enables the perfectly pointed toe.

I am very lonely in college.

My sense of isolation doesn't just apply to women. My only male friend at school is my cousin, Hubie. Many nights, we get high and talk into the wee hours. Hubie confesses that he feels lost, and is in desperate need of something that will make his life make sense. I never say it out loud, but I understand exactly how Hubie feels. Hubie has been on a search for a solution; he's tried shrinks, seminars, various self-help groups, and lots of psychedelics, with no relief. Finally, one day, Hubie announces that he's found the answer—Scientology. Hubie is eager for me to join, and takes me to a kind of Scientology gathering, filled with converts who look like extras from the movie, *Children of the Damned*, with spooky, dead eyes. I decline the invitation to join. Soon, it seems that Hubie's personality has been not just altered, but removed. Everything that made him interesting and unique is gone. He changes so profoundly that I don't know him anymore. After a while, we stop having anything to do with each other. It's a painful loss, but I'm practiced at drowning feelings like that.

25

ICE CREAM MAN

In the summer before my junior year in college, I return home to Chicago, where my first stop is Etta's new place. Advancing age and arthritis has caused Etta to retire, and mom has somehow scored for Etta a gorgeous lakefront apartment in a high-rise peopled with Jewish senior citizens. Etta's apartment has a million dollar view, and is decorated with mom's old, but still beautiful, furniture. Etta is attired in mom's discarded designer clothing. Looking like a Nubian queen, Etta takes me down to the dayroom, full of old folks playing cards, where she introduces me to everyone as "her son." None of the oldsters bat an eye. Many of them gush to me about my wonderful "mom."

One steamy night in Chicago, Abe and I seek the cool of a movie theater, where we see Martin Scorsese's *Taxi Driver*. I am completely blown away and deeply impacted. Even though I have absolutely no knowledge of filmmaking, I become obsessed with the idea of making a take-off on *Taxi Driver* which I will call *Ice Cream Man*.

Fueled by my own manic energy, I talk the son of a friend of mom's into loaning me his state-of-the-art, Super-8 sound camera, I write a script with Abe's assistance, I assemble a cast containing friends, family members, and elevator men, and most importantly, I get a job as an ice cream man. This gives me the essential prop, an ice cream truck, along with an all-white uniform and hat. I actually do a little work at the job, but only enough hours selling ice cream (and pot) to placate my boss. The rest of the time is devoted to making the movie. Mom's luxurious apartment is the perfect place from which to oversee the production, providing a stocked fridge, unlimited phone calls, and a wealth of "costumes" appropriated from mom's and Seymour's clothes closets.

About a week into the shoot, my cousin Johan, who works on the movie, drives me home. We listen to jazz. Johan has become, at sixteen, a superb guitarist, with his own jazz combo. I'm into scat-singing, the kind Ella Fitzgerald has perfected, and I scat along with the music in the car. Johan suggests I should sit in with his combo at the bar where they play. Whether or not he's joking, I am extremely flattered, and take him up on his offer.

The night I am to scat in public, I sit at the bar, and seeing all the people there, I become terrified. I drink to calm my nerves, trying to achieve the sweet spot of well-lubricated but still coherent. I wind up shooting way past it. When I'm called to the stage for the song with my solo, I indicate that I can't make it from my chair to the stage, so a microphone is brought to me. Johan's combo launches into the tune. When Johan gives me my cue, I start scatting. With my eyes closed at first, I think I'm feeling my way into the song. But when I open my eyes, I see the people's reactions, which range from amused to horrified to laughing out loud. I'm rattled. I lose control of my voice. Finally, I sustain the highest note I can hit, drop the mic, and escape out the door.

Stumbling home from my catastrophic musical debut, I have a thought—wouldn't it be funny to enter my apartment building with my pants down around my ankles, wearing no underwear. It *is* funny. At least the doorman seems to get a kick out of it. Then I hear the parking garage door open, followed by the unmistakable sound of my mom's voice. I struggle to pull my pants up, but in my drunken state, I tumble to the floor of the lobby, on my back, and struggle like a turtle, trying to right myself. Mom enters the lobby with Seymour and another couple, Ruth and Stan. Mom spots me flailing around on the floor, smashed, with my pants around my ankles. She goes crazy, and starts to kick at me with her high heels, while bellowing.

"You animal! How could you do this? What is wrong with you?"

"Animal!" Seymour chimes in.

Mom says, over her shoulder, to the other couple.

"Ruth, Stan, I'm so sorry you have to see this."

"It's kind of entertaining," Stan offers.

"Shut up, Stan," Ruth scolds. Mom stomps, and continues to scream.

"Vile pig! Boor! Neanderthal! You're just like that lousy father of yours."

"Animal!" Seymour lends more support.

"You're going to hurt him," Ruth worries.

"I'm gonna *kill* him!" mom corrects Ruth.

"Kill the animal!" Seymour urges.

Instead, the animal is kicked out of his home, onto the street.

2 6
ICE CREAM MAN—PART TWO

I move into a seedy hotel with the star of *Ice Cream Man*, my old high school friend, Roman. Getting booted from my posh digs and base of operations makes the already challenging film production almost impossible. But the show must go on. My mania ramps up a few notches, and I throw myself into the task at hand, with abandon. Lots of people become involved in the production, and they seem to be having fun. I am the guy in charge, and everyone does what I tell them to. My ego is doing backflips.

I even decide to act in the movie, taking a role based on Harvey Keitel's pimp character from *Taxi Driver*. My six-year-old sister, Liza, plays the hooker. My aunt Carolyn has a cameo as a chainsaw-wielding maniac. I've written the female lead as a dancer, allowing me to audition lots of young women, and their feet.

Roman is totally obsessed with professional wrestling, so I write that element into his character. We all take a car ride to

Milwaukee to see and film a night of pro wrestling. Filming the wrestling is strictly forbidden, so I hide the camera in my coat, and sit in between a couple hefty crew members. But, I'm caught filming by some security goons, and I'm hustled into the dark, smelly office of the tough guy in charge. Surrounded by gigantic, mean-looking wrestlers with greased bodies, the tough guy interrogates me.

"What the fuck's the matter with you? Can't you read?"

"Yes sir, I can read."

"Did you not see all the signs that say no photography or filming?"

"I must have missed those."

"Give me one reason why I shouldn't have my boys here kick the livin' crap outta you."

I'm scared to death, but I manage to channel my best Eddie Haskell.

"First, let me say, it's an honor to meet you, sir, and may I tell you, I've loved professional wrestling since I was a little boy, and used to watch with my dad…my departed dad. Now, I'm not going to use the excuse that I have a brain tumor, a terminal one. What I did was wrong. I shouldn't have filmed the wrestling. I just wanted to have something to watch when I can't get out of bed anymore. Before I, you know, leave this world."

The tough guy just stares at me, shakes his head, starts chuckling.

"You're good, kid. You're going places. Now, get the fuck outta here."

The making of *Ice Cream Man* continues. The kid who loaned me the movie camera keeps calling me, begging for his camera back, but I don't return his calls. Finally, toward the end of the shoot, after a long day of directing, mom calls me to come home. I'm relieved, thinking I'm going to be allowed to move back home. But that's not why she called. Upon entering our apartment, I find the camera-kid's parents sitting in the living room with mom and Seymour. None of them are happy with me. They demand the return of the movie camera. And it's a wrap.

I manage to edit the footage into a complete film, and we screen it for delighted viewers all over Chicago's near north side. Even mom has to admit it's pretty good. But, the mania that drives my outrageous behavior and creativity can be exhausting, and sometimes I feel like I'm eating myself alive.

With *Ice Cream Man* in the can, I am compelled to make another film. I *have* to. I turn to cousin Johan, who is not only a musician, but a fine martial artist, and we write a script together. The film we make is called, *Instead of the Dragon*, and stars Johan as a cross between James Bond and Bruce Lee. The character is impeccably attired, takes his vodka shaken not stirred, surrounds himself with beautiful woman, but he's always barefooted, and kicks lots of bad guy ass. For supporting roles, we cast friends, elevator men, and a couple of trophy wives of rich men who know mom. I borrow another movie camera from another sucker, and we're in business. During the shoot, I get a real kick out of choreographing and shooting fight scenes. In the end, *Instead of the Dragon* is not going to win any awards, but directing violence gives me an enormous vicarious thrill—an acceptable outlet for my rage.

27
RISING SUN

I return to college for my junior year. The school offers year-abroad study programs, and after mulling over the options, I decide to go to Japan. I have no idea why. I make the decision very late, so I have no time to learn the language, like the other students have. Arriving in the land of the rising sun, I am entirely unable to communicate, but the place seems to be made for me—I am totally anonymous, taller than I've ever been, and drinking (mostly by men) is practically a national pastime. On the weekends, the packed-like-sardines subway train is overflowing with dark-suited businessmen, many of whom are obviously and unashamedly, sloppy drunk. I'm home.

A Japanese family has been chosen for me to live with, in the gorgeous, shrine and garden-filled city of Kyoto. Whoever made the choice is a genius. My Japanese "father," who likes to be called "Boss," is a colorful, lovable drunk, his sweet wife is a great cook, and the aging grandma farts prodigiously, and insists on watching me bathe in the tub. My fourteen-year-old "brother," Harushige and his eight-year-old sister, Junko are priceless. On my third day there, I wake up to find them snuggled on either side of me in bed (the traditional tatami mat). I am told that this is a demonstration of "Amaeru," which means the wish to be loved.

Almost every night, after dinner, Boss has me join him in the attic to drink giant bottles of sake. Boss's English is as bad as my Japanese, so we communicate using drawings on a big chalkboard. The drunker we get, the more licentious our chalk drawings become. Boss draws an octopus waving fans in its tentacles. Then, he adds another octopus. Finally, he draws them having sex. Boss is an accomplished artist. When I draw vivid pictures of octopi fucking humans, Boss is delighted beyond description.

My own sex life in Japan is not nearly as exciting as that of the octopi. Expectations of hot geisha girls and bound feet never come close to fruition. Even when my ability to speak the language improves, it's a real challenge to find a willing partner. And when I do, the general submissiveness I encounter gets boring fast.

I am commissioned to make a documentary about an American woman working in a Japanese orphanage in Kyoto. After this rewarding experience, comes the highlight of the year. The college has set up an internship for me with the great

Japanese film director, Masahiro Shinoda, in Tokyo. I learn much from Shinoda-san, and he tells me about a cinema art house very near my apartment in Tokyo. When the internship is finished, I walk to the art house almost every day and watch movies. These classic movies are either in Japanese, or they're foreign language films with Japanese subtitles. It's a challenge sitting in the theater, trying to figure out the movies' plots. By far, my favorite films are the ones by Buster Keaton and Charlie Chaplin; not only are they completely brilliant, there are no subtitles or dialogue to have to deal with—storytelling in its purest form.

Afterwards, I hang out in jazz coffee shops, where I practice my Japanese on people trying to listen to the music, and then at night, the riotous ritual of drinking and drawing with my Japanese father, Boss. When I return to the homeland, after a year abroad, it seems that the main thing I take away from my experience in Japan is an ability to show off at sushi bars.

28
ACTION!

Back from Japan, in my senior year of college, I enroll in a film class, with the alluring title, "Cinema and Celebration; The Structure of Ecstasy." I make a few short films, the most ambitious of which I call *Pedalogic*. This film depicts a day in the life of a female foot; waking up, chased by an evil sock, surrounded by other feet at dance class, and finally, a slow-motion shower of talcum powder. I'm proud of the film, and shocked by the universally negative reaction; I am thought by many to be grossly insensitive because the teacher of the film class has only one foot. I hadn't considered that.

The total rejection of my work, and therefore of me, is devastating. Filled with anger and resentment, I overreact, and leave school a few credits short of a degree. The pain of this experience serves to fuel my already surging ambition. I have caught the film bug in a major way, and am now intent on becoming not simply a working filmmaker, but a "Great Director."

I am accepted into one of L.A.'s top film schools. At my interview, I screen my foot film for the head honchos. They claim to like it, but probably not as much as the steep tuition my mother will be paying. This is a serious, highly demanding school, and the rigors force me to give up extracurriculars like booze and drugs.

In the summer before the start of film school, I meet Greta, a lovely girl with lovely feet. I'm crazy about her, and together, we find a cozy bungalow in Santa Monica, where we embark on the closest thing to a real relationship I've ever known. This idyllic situation doesn't last long. Greta wants to get married, but she soon realizes that I am already married, to my single-minded dream of being the next Orson Welles. Greta moves out, freeing me to pursue my quest, unencumbered by love.

For three years at film school, I work harder than I ever have; learning the technical aspects of filmmaking, studying the masters, screenwriting, and making short films. One my favorite shorts is a film I make with an old friend, Atticus, the son of one of mom's best friends, who recently moved out to L.A. Atticus is a few years younger, and I've known him since he was a child. Atticus is an accomplished sailor, and takes me sailing in the Pacific. Dad would love him. Atticus is going into the Merchant Marines, and says he'd really like to be in a film of mine before he departs. I ask him what he can do. Atticus thinks about it, and says, "I'm pretty good at being short."

So, I write *High Steppin'*, a story about a little guy who can't get girls because he's short; after a series of romantic rejections, we see him walking down the street in a long black cloak—he's now over eight feet tall. He meets a girl, and takes her dancing to a club, where he keeps hitting his head on a disco ball. They go back to her place, but he is too tall to pass through the doorway, at which point, the guy on whose shoulders the little fellow has been sitting, emerges from the cloak for the first time, and starts flirting with the girl. Unable to compete, the little guy leaves, trailing his long cloak behind him. Finally, the girl tires of the other guy, and goes back to the little guy. It's a happy ending, which is unusual for me. Atticus is superb, and the film wins some awards. The film's theme, that one's insides are more important than their outsides, is an idea I would not actually embrace for many years.

Making film after film, my ambition soars, culminating in my thesis film *Parting Shot*, at the time, the longest student film ever made, at forty-nine minutes. Financed by the meager inheritance I receive from my dad, *Parting Shot* is a pitch black comedy about a father-and-son relationship, in which the father tricks the son into shooting him to death.

While I'm editing the film, mom visits from Chicago, and screens a rough cut of her son's masterwork. She is extremely impressed, and insists on hosting a "premiere" in Chicago. After a screening at film school, the movie garners a glowing LA Times review, "Parting Shot is fresh, focused, and passionate movie making." Ecstatic, I drive around town and steal a ton of LA Times from newspaper vending machines, forgetting there's something called Xerox.

Then, it's on to Chicago, where mom, ever the socialite, has orchestrated a splashy, Hollywood-style premiere at a trendy, Gold Coast movie theater; a catered affair with an open bar and passed hors d'oeuvres. In an expression of mother-love-overkill, she even gets my name placed on the theater's marquis, in gigantic letters. The invited guests are the city's elite. With all the fur coats, it looks like the set of *Wild Kingdom*. I am mortified at how over-the-top everything is. It gets worse during the screening, when I am reminded that my film is dark and twisted and intensely *personal*, not exactly this crowd's cup of tea. Finally, the whole thing is just too much for me; I leave in mid-screening, go out to the now-empty lobby, grab a bottle of wine, and drop onto a bench. I am followed into the lobby by my old pal Abe, who had come out to L.A. to help on the film, and also manages this theater. Abe sits down beside me, takes a big swig from my bottle.

"Hey, Maestro, wanna tell me what the fuck you're doin' out here?" Abe asks.

"They hate it," I moan.

"They *love* it, they're pissing themselves, laughing at all the right places."

"Not that asshole who keeps checking his Rolex."

"Who?"

"The rich fuck."

"That describes everybody here, except you and me."

"The picture looks shitty, so grainy. Like I filmed it in a blizzard."

"That's what happens when you project sixteen millimeter in a real theater. Maybe you should'a had the screening in your bathroom."

"I never should'a let my mom talk me into this. What a disaster."

"Man, what's wrong with you, this is the greatest night of your life!"

"It's fucked."

"You're fucked."

"You're fucked."

"Fine, we're both fucked. I'm going back in, see how this crappy movie ends. You just stay out here and see if you can suck every ounce of pleasure out of this thing."

Abe goes back into the theater. I go back into my bottle.

29
SOLO ACT

Eager to launch my Hollywood career, I once again leave school a few credits shy of graduating. Completely on my own for the first time at the age of twenty-four, I'm at an almost total loss. I can mix a mean martini and tastefully decorate a living room, but that's pretty much the extent of my practical knowledge.

Nevertheless, I remain supremely confident in my talent. In my grandiose view, I see myself as a great artist—an opinion no one else in town seems to share. There is a vast difference between who I am, and who I think I am. Perhaps, that explains the pain and outrage I feel when, initially, no one in Hollywood shows the slightest interest in me. I had assumed that my student film would put me on the map, and serve as a calling card. But I can't get anyone to see it; one producer even asks to screen a trailer instead of the film—a trailer for a student film.

Work is impossible to find. I blame film school for not preparing me for the real world. When someone tells me that's bullshit, I blame my parents. I see other guys from my film school getting work, but it's lowly work, stuff I'd never do. Emotionally, I vacillate between Ego, whose message is, "These Hollywood fuckers will be sorry for ignoring me," and Fear, which screams, "I have no talent, I'm hopelessly doomed!" Fear usually wins out, and I gravitate to the worst case scenario. In one particular scenario, my brain produces vivid images of future me walking freeway meridians with a cardboard sign that reads, "Will Direct for Food." I seem to get off on scaring the shit out of myself. I am never more creative than when I'm concocting horrifying scenes of my future. If only I could harness this creative energy, I'd be a multi-millionaire. But the crushing, present reality is that I'm penniless and drowning in a self-made cocktail of fear, rejection and resentment, which can only be addressed by a return to the bottle and blow.

The cavalry finally arrives in the form of a producer who does see my thesis film, and hires me as the second unit director on a feature film. Working for three months in Santa Fe, New Mexico is the perfect tonic for my blues; the terrain around Santa Fe, where we shoot, is incredibly picturesque. I get to hire my own crew, five pals from film school. We are given a ratty house to live in, but we're just happy to be involved in the making of a Hollywood movie. Being wasted everyday doesn't seem to adversely affect the results I produce. I find myself directing scenes with horses and motorcycles and accomplished actors. This is the real deal. I feel part of something. I meet a girl at a bar who deals cocaine. She invites me to stay at her place, pissing off my crew.

The film's producer, the one who hired me based on my student film, wants to have a big screening of my film. I'm thrilled to have everyone working on the feature see my work. At the screening, everyone gets shit-faced, and talks loudly, as though my film is some sort of background entertainment. I can't hide my disappointment, so I get thoroughly drunk, and I allow the screening to tarnish this mostly excellent adventure.

3 0
WALK ON BEACH

Hardly any work comes my way after the Santa Fe film, but hobnobbing with the cast and crew winds up providing me entree into the Hollywood party scene, where I try to play the happening young hyphenate. Free booze, cocaine, and appetizers, what could be better? How 'bout a ravishing, young actress; her name is Dana, and she doesn't drink, but she does buy my bullshit, for a while. She allows me to kiss, fondle, and worship her feet, but says she isn't comfortable with anything beyond that.

Dana is offered a meaty role in a high profile film, but she's worried about having to do nudity. I impress upon her that this is the kind of opportunity that can make her career. She finally accepts the role, and asks me to hang out in her trailer on the set, and help her run lines. Then, suddenly, I am no longer needed, and Dana stops returning my calls. I drive to her home late one night, with a major buzz on. There's a strange car in her driveway, a Porsche. I crawl through the bushes, and peer through Dana's bedroom window, where she is enthusiastically performing oral sex on the male star of the film. Easy come…

Unsuccessfully trying to find work, I get the distinct feeling that people see me as something less than a wunderkind, so I start to "pad my resume." This involves embellishment, enhancement, and downright lying—even when lying isn't necessary—almost for sport. I meet a woman at a bar who seems to be interested in me. She wears open-toed shoes, and I sense real promise. She asks me about myself.

"So, what do you do?"

"I'm a writer and a director."

"Really? What have you done?"

"Oh, lots of stuff."

"Like what?"

"Well…I just finished a screenplay that Jack Lemmon is attached to star in."

"I don't think so."

"Excuse me?"

"I'm Jack Lemmon's manager."

I am taken aback, momentarily.

"Really, well, Jack just probably hasn't told you about it yet. The project is pretty hush hush."

"*Jack* tells me *everything*. I know what he had for breakfast this morning."

"Look, if Jack doesn't trust you, that's not my problem."

"You have other problems, buddy. The kinds that require a psychoanalyst."

She gets off her bar stool. Sets down her half-finished long island ice tea.

"Thanks for the drink."

And she leaves the bar. I finish her drink, and order another.

Not having much luck with women at bars or parties, I have to think outside the box. In a time before online dating, there was a service in a newspaper called "The Personals," in which seekers of companionship record self-introductions, and supply contact info. Trying to cover all the bases, I describe myself in my intro as an "International Entrepreneur and Jewish Big Brother." I listen to recordings of many women; regarding "interests," a very common choice is "Walks on the beach." This perks my interest—beach suggests feet. One woman, for whom English is obviously a second language, keeps repeating, "Walk on beach, fine dining, jewelry store, walk on beach, fine dining, jewelry store…"

Not a single woman reaches out to the International Entrepreneur/Jewish Big Brother, but I contact three "Walk on Beach" gals to see if they'd like to walk on the beach with me. The first one whines, "I hate beaches, they're so dirty." The second says she meant *Miami* Beach. Our final contestant actually goes to the beach with me. She's nice, but one second toe is considerably longer than the other, and I have to resist the urge to clip it.

31
BABY MOGUL

Mom announces that she's coming out to the coast to visit her "Baby Mogul." The last thing in the world I want is for my mom to see the reality of my life; how far from a mogul I actually am. My aunt Carolyn is aware of my situation. I'm okay with having her know. Aunt Carolyn encourages me, feeds me occasionally, and takes me to buy furniture, where I even get to pick out a lamp. But, for my mom's visit, I stage an alternate reality—I keep her away from my crummy apartment by claiming it's being fumigated, I borrow a friend's new BMW, with a promise to detail it, and I talk Dana into pretending to be my girlfriend, in exchange for unlimited help learning her lines.

Having a woman like Dana on my arm is sure to make mom think I'm a happening player. It is also likely to bring out mom's salty side—she has detested every girlfriend I've ever had, from eighth grade on. She scrutinizes them mercilessly—"She's not well educated…from a bad family…not Jewish…*too* Jewish…can't tell a salad fork from a dinner fork." No one is good enough for her son.

Mom makes reservations for the three of us at an upscale Beverly Hills restaurant. One great thing about mom is that she can really drink, so I've always felt comfortable drinking around her. Dana looks dazzling, but true to form, mom can't stand her (too thin, not cultured, chews with mouth open). Mom makes no attempt to hide her disdain, providing for Dana, a terribly uncomfortable evening, and for me, a little payback for Dana dumping me earlier.

At the end of mom's visit, I drive her to the airport in my friend's car.

"What is this, a Mercedes?" mom asks me.

"It's a BMW."

"Those are good, too. You know, I have to admit, I was a little worried about you, with all your troubles and everything. Show business is a tough nut to crack, even if you're perfectly fine. Lots of people would be struggling, but not my little mogul."

"Nope."

"I hope you don't mind me saying, this girl, this Darla—"

"Dana," I correct her.

"Whatever. She's not a keeper. Might help open a few doors, but no kind of permanent fixture."

"Very astute."

We drive in silence for a while, then mom remembers something.

"Oh, I almost forgot. Seymour sends his love."

I laugh out loud.

"What's funny?"

"Nothing, mom, what airline are you on?"

"United…you'll send me your Jack Lemmon script, when you're finished?"

"You'll be the first, mom."

We park at the airport. I walk mom to the gate. She departs and I hit the airport bar for a few, much-needed cocktails. Making such an effort to appear successful really heightens my sense of failure. I want so badly to tell mom the truth about my life, but it simply wouldn't be acceptable.

32

SOMETHING TO HIDE

As my career struggles increase, so does my drinking and drug use. What is most exhausting is my ongoing attempt to hide these habits. So much energy is devoted to trying to keep secret the extent of my indulgence. I search for a kind of alcohol that can't be detected on one's breath, finally settling on vodka, supposedly the only liquor that doesn't smell. And just in case vodka *does* smell, I keep in my car's glove compartment, a stash of various brands of gum, Tic-Tacs, Lifesavers, and portable breath sprays. I obscure my tell-tale eyes behind designer sunglasses, worn constantly, and placed in a variety of strategic locations. I even take my driver's license photo at the DMV looking overtly wasted, so if a cop stops me driving, I'll match the photo.

This preoccupation with hiding increases my irritability. I become easily agitated and edgy; I get into arguments, conflicts, fights. Everyone else is always to blame, as I burn bridge after bridge. I sabotage jobs, fire agents, and am fired by agents. Almost all of my actions are self-destructive, which leads to way less than stellar earnings.

My old film school offers me a job teaching screenwriting. The pay is so paltry that only a particular kind of person is willing to do this—someone independently wealthy or someone pretty broke. I usually show up to class coked up, and I'm surprised to discover how enjoyable teaching is. I am the "cool" teacher who goes out drinking with students after class. I teach for almost a year, then, as my own career takes on even more water, I become preoccupied with warning my students about how awful the film business is. I think I'm doing them a real service, but the administration doesn't quite see it that way, and I am unceremoniously let go.

A dirty little secret of mine is that I support my income by selling valuable objects I inherited from my father; I sell a nautical antique from a Spanish galleon to a movie producer who is a big partier…a guy named Guy who wants to be known as "*The* Guy." He gives me a job that involves doing rewrites on screenplays he's acquired, scoring drugs, and hanging out. I see myself as a kind of Tom Hagen consigliere figure from The Godfather. It's a pretty cushy gig until he fires me, for stealing a couple cases of champagne from a wrap party. This is a dude who can afford to lose an ocean of champagne. I ratchet up the ill will when I get caught making threatening prank calls to The Guy after he canned me.

When I think of all the stuff I did for that creep…in addition to rewriting his lousy scripts, I picked up his kids at school, went to the cleaners, got his Jaguar washed, and made sure his wife never found out about all the bimbos he was *shtupping*. The Guy told me he was my mentor, that I was like a son to him, then he fires my ass—what a phony! Hollywood is full of nothing but phonies…says the pseudo-writer of Jack Lemon movies, with the fake girlfriend.

33
ROYAL FLUSH

I don't know how exactly, but I do manage to score an occasional job: directing a commercial or an industrial film, doing a rewrite or a script polish, and once in a blue moon, a real quality gig falls into my lap.

My film school classmate and friend, a French guy named Philippe, asks me to direct a film that he's producing about the Cannes Film Festival. I'm excited about going to France, and absolutely thrilled that Philippe has worked tirelessly to arrange for me to conduct an on-camera interview at the festival with one of my all-time favorite directors, the great Billy Wilder.

The night before the Wilder interview, I'm nervous, and I decide to calm myself with a wee bit of bar drinking. Once I take the first drink, I can never control my intake, and this evening turns into a full night of club-hopping. I go home very late and very sloshed, with a local woman, and I oversleep the next day. No one from the film is able to contact me, and I miss the interview with Wilder. Philippe is enraged. He berates me in French, in front of the crew, then sends me home, to the states.

Ruining relationships with my thoughtless and unprofessional behavior is becoming a pattern of mine, one I can't seem to break. A high school buddy from Chicago, Willis, who worked on my first filmmaking effort, *Ice Cream Man*, hires me to direct a documentary about the Poker Championship of the World in Las Vegas (years before the televised poker shows). Another quality project with a fascinating subject matter, *Poker Town* features the top one-hundred poker players in the world, vying for a winner-take-all pot of one million dollars (a lot of money in those days). The stars of our film are cinematic; colorful personalities, hope-to-die gamblers, thrill junkies.

The shoot is going well; I'm behaving myself, and doing a nice job with the interviews (these are addicts, after all), until I'm approached by one of the poker players who wants more screen time, in exchange for a copious amount of cocaine. It's a no brainer. For my next on-camera interview, with the number one poker player in the world, Stu Unger, I show up coked out of my mind. My rapid-fire, incoherent babbling is too much even for Stu, a celebrated coke fiend. I am ushered out of the room, then out of town. And I fold on another opportunity and friendship.

3 4
BAD BOY

When it comes to romance, I am becoming that guy you *don't* want to take home to mother. Some women are attracted to me as a "bad boy," but the badder I get, the less attractive they find me. In truth, I desperately crave closeness with a woman, but at the same time, my fear of intimacy is overwhelming. I am dogged by a mounting terror of being known. I can't bear the thought of someone getting close enough to see my real rotten self, then agreeing with my lowly self-assessment. My drinking and drugging start to drive women away. I am accused, more than once, of being a drunk, which I always deny, and after which, I act like I've been wounded by the slight. In the odd case that I do achieve something close to closeness with a woman, I invariably manipulate my partner into initiating a breakup, allowing me to play my new favorite role, victim.

I wake up one afternoon with a porn actress whose work I was a fan of a decade ago. She laughs as she describes my behavior the previous night: apparently, at a local Jack in the Box drive-thru, I drunkenly beat the plastic clown/speaker to smithereens with a baseball bat when the clown couldn't get my order right. I have absolutely no memory of this episode, but I pretend I do, and I laugh along with her. It's amusing the first time, but as I start experiencing blackouts regularly, there's nothing funny about it. The blackouts get my attention like nothing ever has.

Hiding my alcohol intake is no longer enough. I have to *control* it. I attempt a number of different strategies: only drinking wine and beer, hanging out with non-drinkers, hiding booze and drugs far away from home, figuring that when I feel the urge, I won't have the will. Then there's limiting the number of drinks, never drinking alone, never drinking at home, only drinking at home, and finally, cold turkey, which lasts a few hours, at most. When none of these strategies work, after what I consider to have been an honest effort, my delusional mind gives me the green light to drink and drug the way I used to, and I do, with a renewed vengeance, and more denial than ever.

Mom is turning fifty, and I travel to Chicago for her surprise birthday party. Mom is not at all surprised, and she clearly doesn't like the gift I give her, a framed photo of me. Seymour makes a sloppy, embarrassing toast, and everyone in the family vies for who can be most vicious. In my few days home, I try to cover all the bases: I visit Etta, bearing a six-pack of her favorite, Budweiser (knowing she will only drink one). We watch a White Sox game together. Etta's arthritic fingers can hardly operate the remote. I party with a few old drinking buddies, none of whom are as far gone as me. I hang out with my little sisters, Liza and Jewel, where, in the depths of my depravity, I turn my sisters' sixteen-year-old friends on to cocaine. I imagine that these girls look at me in awe, as I expertly chop the lines of coke. What a guy.

I check out Amy's modest, new apartment. I peruse the place, and try to be nice and complimentary.

"Lovely. Spacious. Great view. Hey, we need to toast your new place. Got anything to drink?"

Amy cautiously opens a bottle of wine, pours a couple of glasses. I lift my glass.

"To Amy's new abode. May it always be...up to code."

"I see you haven't lost that brilliant wit," Amy comments, sarcastically.

I take a big sip of wine. Amy takes a little sip. As we sit at her kitchen table, talking, I become increasingly more bothered that Amy is leaving most of the wine in her glass. People who don't finish their drinks is something that has always disturbed me. Now, I try hard not to finish mine. Finally, I just have to. I grab the bottle, tilt it toward Amy.

"Come on, finish, so I can pour us another."

Amy doesn't touch her glass. She just stares accusingly at me.

"What?" I ask.

"I'm worried about you, Duff."

"I'm fine."

"Your hands shake. You slur your words. You…you remind me of dad."

"Yeah, well, you remind me of…Chumley."

"Who the hell is Chumley?"

"That walrus on the Tennessee Tuxedo cartoon show."

"You're not well."

Back in L.A, it's impossible not to be inundated with the spectacle of guys in hot cars, with hot women. I resent these undeserving trust-fund fuckers and entitled young sheiks, but they may be on to something. Embracing my long-held belief that something on the outside can fix what's wrong inside, I trade in my clunker for a "pre-owned" Alfa Romeo Spider convertible I can't afford, hoping it will be a chick magnet. I then drive drunk through stop signs and red lights for months, without getting a single scratch on the Spider, or a single chick into it.

35
FINISH ME

The power of denial is undeniable, but I can't deny the fact that booze and drugs are taking a punishing toll on my body. Once a fairly well-muscled jock, I'm now a shriveled, loose-skinned slug. I won't even look in the mirror anymore. I find myself gasping for breath at even the slightest exertion. Just *watching* sports is exhausting. I can't get motivated to exercise, except for the couple times a month I manage to drag myself onto the tennis court. Tennis is the perfect sport for me, especially singles, where you're only dealing with one other person, and they are far away, across net.

There's a woman I hit with, Carrie, a decent tennis player, older than me, with a kind of weathered look, but still somewhat attractive. I've been giving her the "come here/go away" routine for months. Frustrated that I haven't asked her out on a date, Carrie invites me to her place for dinner. I show up with a couple bottles of wine, downing a bottle alone beforehand.

Carrie has an irritating southern accent which reminds me of Blanche Dubois from *Streetcar Named Desire*. She feeds me a southern meal, after which she leads me to her canopied bed, where I finally get a look at her feet. They're covered with red bumps and blotches. I almost gag. Carrie says, "It's just turf toe," as if it's no big deal. I'm almost angry. I take it personally, as if she intentionally withheld her feet until it was too late. And it *is* too late. I can't back out now. I'm too far down the road to doing the deed.

In the midst of it, I feel a violent rage, which I think isn't just about her feet. Carrie screams out, "Finish me!" I've never heard that before. I think, "'Finish me?' What the hell does that mean? Does she want me to kill her? I'll gladly oblige. That's what you get for hiding those awful feet. I'll finish you." Afterward, Carrie wants me to join her in the shower. I tell her I'll join her only if she wears her socks in the shower. She refuses. I forcibly put her socks on her feet, throw her into the shower, and join her, barely able to contain my fury.

Driving home, in a rare moment of self-reflection, I ask myself where this rage is coming from? I really frightened an innocent woman, and myself, as well. This is a level of anger and potential violence I've never experienced before. I'm shaken. I no longer trust myself around women. I decide I'm done with dating. "Finish Me" finishes me.

36
BURNING DESIRE

At a Hollywood bar I frequent called Ports, I'm a very minor celebrity due to my uncanny ability to guess women's shoe sizes. The appeal of this establishment is that it's walking distance from my place, extremely dark, and most importantly, I can almost always find a stool at the bar. I can't emphasize enough the importance of a stool. The longer my drinking career lasts, remaining upright, for even brief periods of time, becomes a challenge. I am seriously intent on inventing a product I call "Port-a-Stool." I make drawings and designs, and I look into patents. But like most of my plans, it goes nowhere.

One dark night at Ports, I sit on a stool at the bar, and decide to hit the washroom for a quick toot of coke. I ask the guy next to me to save my seat. He agrees. When I exit the washroom, the guy who was sitting next to me is gone, and my stool is occupied by someone else. I approach the stool thief.

"Excuse me, that's my stool you're sitting on." The guy turns around. He's big. He looks at me, just laughs in my face, and turns back around.

"Look, pal, I'm trying to be civil about this."

"I'm not your pal," the Big Guy huffs.

"I don't like talking about this, but I suffer from lumber spinal stenosis. It may be terminal. I get excruciating pain when I have to stand, even for short periods of time."

The Big Guy tosses a handful of change at my feet.

"Here, buy yourself an operation, and get the fuck outta my face."

"It's *my* stool!"

"Don't make me come down there, asshole."

"Come on down, I'll kick your fat ass."

The Big Guy and everyone at the bar burst out laughing. A patron at the bar interjects.

"Just give the poor guy his fucking stool."

"No. It's *my* stool," the Big Guy insists.

"Bullshit! I've been here for hours, sitting on *that* stool. I asked a guy to save my seat when I had to go to the washroom..."

"Yeah, I see what you were doing in there." The Big Guy pantomimes crazily snorting coke. I glance in the mirror behind the bar, and wipe the powder off my nose.

"Fucking narc," I hiss.

"Fucking loser fag drug addict," he hisses back.

"You're the fag," I counter. I pause, gaze longingly at my stool, compose myself, and lower my voice.

"Hey, man, can't we just be reasonable here?"

"Here's reasonable."

The Big Guy blows the foamy head of his beer at me. It lands on my face and shirt. He turns back around. I'd like to smash my glass over his head, but don't want to waste the booze, so I gather up a few sheets of newspaper, and when the Big Guy leans forward, I place the newspaper under his ass. I then take my lighter and set the newspaper ablaze. His jacket catches on fire. A quick-thinking patron dowses the jacket. The Big Guy is okay, and I am kicked out of Ports, forever. Now, I mostly drink at home, alone.

My twenty-seventh birthday is a rough one; I haven't directed a feature film by the age of twenty-six, like Spielberg and Orson Welles, as I always vowed I would. How did I ever think I was in their league? I am, as a teacher once dubbed me, a "chronic underachiever." Maybe it has something to do with the fact that my top priority in life is getting high, and screw everything else. It is not really a *chosen* priority. I frequently choose not to drink, but when the urge seizes me, I *have* to obey it, and I *always* wind up drinking. I've reached the point where if I have to choose between food and booze, every time I choose booze. I can no longer hide *or* control my drinking and drugging. I go on job interviews in an obviously altered state. I have become unemployed and unemployable. And I'm running out of dad's treasures to sell.

Cousin Buzz and Abe have become successful producers. That's hard enough to deal with, but I've also been furious at them for not helping me more, when the truth is they've both given me many opportunities over the years. For me, nothing is enough.

Now, Cousin Buzz, aware of my sorry state, throws me a bone, a job writing a script for a sitcom; no chance to embarrass myself on the set, just sit alone and write, which I think I can still do. After I finish the script, the production office sends me the rewrite. After reading it, I go ballistic, deciding that my script has been ruined. I am fully aware that when a writer turns in a script for a show, it *always* gets rewritten, but I storm into the office anyway, demanding to know "who the fuck fucked up my script?" I lose it, and throw a tantrum, insulting the other writers, producers, and their families. I burn the last bridge standing. The other writers and producers stare at me in total disbelief, none of them has ever watched someone commit career suicide, right in front of them.

37

CRASHING

I get dragged to a high school reunion for people who wound up in L.A, where, between gulps of spiked punch, I spot a bunch of "losers" I haven't seen since high school; guys who always had their hands raised in class, and got their work in on time, guys I teased and tortured mercilessly, who now seem comfortable with their normal, modestly successful lives. Maybe it's my imagination, but they seem to look at me like I'm beneath them, like I'm some kind of bum. I look at them, and I can't believe I feel almost jealous. I run into an old school chum, Chris, and I convince him to let me crash at his place. Just in time too, I'm about to be evicted.

My new roommate Chris has an actual job, as a wine buyer for a local chain of grocery stores. Chris fancies himself a wine connoisseur. He brings wine home, swirls it in a glass, sniffs it, and spouts off endlessly about the wine's "bouquet" and "aeration" and "complexity." I'm thinking, "Just pop the fucking cork already!" Chris is out all day, so I just lay around, getting high, and writing screenplays that will never be filmed, or even read. Since my hiatus from dating, I've turned into a minor voyeur. Chris is a lady's man, and when I hear his car pull up after a date with a lady, I hide in his closet, and watch them doing it. It's a delightful diversion until one night, Chris's date hops off the bed, and makes a beeline for the closet, thinking it's the bathroom. I collapse to the floor, but when she opens the closet door, she discovers me. She screams bloody murder, and starts kicking the crap out of me. Chris tells me, in no uncertain terms, that I've got to find somewhere else to crash.

I prevail on another old friend, Artie, my cocaine dealer and a very bad businessman. He's a sweet crackhead, and gives me a couch. Artie is so dizzy he doesn't know that I'm ripping off a gram of coke a day from him…until he does. Artie is outraged, he can't believe I'm stealing from him after he took me in. I apologize profusely, but Artie knows me well enough to know that my apologies are meaningless. He throws me out. I'm bothered by the idea that a hope-to-die crack fiend thinks *I'm* too fucked up.

I rent a shit hole single in Hollywood, where my primary activity is killing cockroaches. I'm drinking round the clock, but to diminishing returns. I have to drink more and more to achieve the desired affect—Blotto. I buy my booze at a number of different liquor stores, so that the guys behind the counter don't think I'm a drunk. My body wakes me up in the middle of night, demanding alcohol. I sleep with a cheap bottle of vodka under my bed. I beg Artie for coke, and the sweet schmuck comes through.

A growing paranoia colors my shrinking world; I sleep with a carrot peeler on the bedside table. Suspecting my phone is bugged, I take the phone completely apart, forgetting that it was disconnected a while ago. Other than booze runs, I hardly ever leave the apartment, but when I do, I think I'm being followed. I don't want anyone to see what I've become. My only human contact is with the mailman, through the slot.

For years, I drank exclusively hi-end booze, like the pricey brands I was weened on from my parents' liquor cabinet. Now, I'll guzzle anything at all, including, in desperate moments, Paco Rabanne cologne.

3 8
GONE

One afternoon, I'm startled awake by a rapping at the door. Nobody ever visits me. I army-crawl to the window, and peak through the dark curtains. It's Cousin Buzz. I let him in. He looks around my place, can't hide his revulsion, but is unusually gentle.

"You doin' okay, Duffer?"

"Not bad."

"Just came by to tell you how sorry I am. We all are."

"Sorry about what?"

"You don't know?"

"Know what?"

"Aw, Jesus. Better sit down."

We both sit.

"Your mom, she passed away. Yesterday. Sudden brain aneurysm. I'm so sorry."

I just sit there, shellshocked, hardly able to speak.

"Nobody told me."

"Probably because you're harder to reach than the Unabomber."

"Fifty-two," I mumble.

"Huh?"

"Mom. She was fifty-two."

Buzz takes out his wallet, opens it, hands me a wad of cash.

"For the flight. You gotta go home, buddy."

On the plane, sucking on little airplane booze bottles, while trying to locate my grief underneath layers of numbness, I have the perverse thought, "I'm in mourning, that means I can drink without public scorn. Nice." And in another warped line of thinking, I imagine myself as a wise and powerful godfather figure, coming home to make everything okay for everyone in my family. Again, such an enormous discrepancy between who I think I am, and who I actually am.

I stay at my sister Amy's place in Chicago, surrounded by waves of grieving family and friends. I desperately want to be a part of the sadness, but I simply can't get to where everyone else is at, in terms of honest emotion. All three of my sisters can't believe what a mess I've become. This is communicated in their expressions of disgust. Luckily, they are too devastated about mom to really focus on me. They can't stop crying. My sister Liza wails.

"First Etta, and now mom…"

Then, Liza looks at me, with disdain.

"And soon, *you'll* be joining them."

The mention of Etta really throws me.

"Etta?!"

"She passed away a couple months ago," Jewel informs me.

"Why the hell didn't you guys let me know?"

Amy won't listen to my crap.

"We couldn't reach you, moron. We tried. I called all fourteen phone numbers I have for you."

The one-two gut punch of mom and Etta leaves me reeling. My legs buckle. I make it over to the bar, and guzzle a big, stiff drink. I wait for its effect. Nothing. I need to have more. Leaning against the bar, I stew on what Amy has told me; that there will be almost no inheritance, just like with dad. I become angry at my parents for raising us in the lap of luxury, never preparing us for life, and then leaving us with nothing. Anger has always been much easier for me to access than sadness.

Later, stumbling through mom's apartment, I gravitate to her shoe closet, and happen upon one of the strangest sights I've ever seen—all three sisters scrounging around amidst a mountain of shoes, trying to fit mom's size six shoes on their size eight or nine feet. I don't know whether to laugh or cry. I laugh, hysterically. Amy is enraged.

"Why don't you just go back to Los Angeles. You're useless. Completely useless."

That single word, "useless" cuts through my entire defense system; my denial, my excuses, my bullshit. It bursts the dam. So often, the end of a drinking and drugging career requires a big and dramatic event—a prison sentence, an overdose, a tragic car accident. In my case, it's a single word.

39
WELCOME TO
THE JUNGLE

Back in Hollywood, I'm at wit's end. I've been consumed by fears all my life; sharks in pools, public speaking, the future, being a fraud, being found out, being a failure, death, and maybe my worst fear of all...that I would grow up to be like my father. I remember, when I was a little boy, seeing my dad passed out on the floor, in a puddle of puke, and vowing I would never be like him. Now, I *am* him.

Utterly lost and hopeless, and convinced my life is over at thirty, I toss back my final drinks, and I drive up to Mulholland, a road overlooking the city, with the serious intention of driving off a cliff. Hurtling up the dark, canyon road, I hear a familiar sound—a siren. After a brief chase, a cop pulls me over, and makes me take a sobriety test, which I fail miserably. The cop arrests me for drunk driving. I'm put into a cell for the night, and the next day, a judge sentences me to six Alcoholics Anonymous meetings.

I skulk into my first meeting, in a church basement, and am descended upon by sober maniacs with teeth too white, and eyes too bright. Somehow, they know I'm a newcomer; perhaps it's my sweating, or shaking, or difficulty keeping the coffee in my cup, or my struggle to not fall off my chair. Everybody seems to know everybody else. It's a mix of people I've never seen in the same place—from skid row denizens to major celebrities, all interacting. And there's something a little crazy about the ambiance…it almost feels like a New Years Eve celebration.

This is a meeting where they go around the room and identify: "I'm Frank, I'm an alcoholic.", "Nancy, I'm an addict." When it gets to me, I say, "I'm Duffy, wrongly convicted drunk driver." This is greeted with uproarious laughter. I despise them all, I hate being laughed at. But later, something else emerges, a sense that these people might know me on some deeper level, and I might know them—the first spark of identification.

I continue to attend meetings after the mandatory six, mainly because I have nothing else to do, and for the free coffee and cookies. I am deeply suspicious of the kindness shown me by the people there. What do they want from me? There's so much strange, new information flying around the rooms, the attendees almost seem to be speaking in a foreign language.

A man with very blue eyes and a serene demeanor approaches me, and strikes up a conversation. This is Stephan, a gay TV actor, who announces at the end of our chat that he will be my sponsor. Fine, whatever that is. Then, Stephan shakes my hand, and doesn't let it go. He stares into my eyes, and says, "We do not drink, we do not use, one day at a time, *no matter what.*"

I just look at him.

"Agreed?" he asks.

"Agreed." I answer.

We shake on it.

40
DRY

As alcohol and drugs slowly exit my system, there appears a gaping hole in my gut. I try to fill it with tubs of Häagen-Dazs, cigarettes, pornography, and binge-watching TV (decades before it's a thing). I even drag myself to a yoga class, hoping that being surrounded by lots of female feet will help to fill the void. It doesn't. Nothing does.

I find myself plagued by the excruciating feelings that drinking had so effectively obliterated; extreme social discomfort, intense anxiety, guilt, remorse, loss. Physically, I'm a wreck; I shake uncontrollably, and sweat profusely. When I shake hands at meetings, the people there pretend not to notice that my hand is soaking wet. I wear sunglasses indoors, not to emulate Jack Nicholson, but because I simply can't stand eye contact. I feel crazier sober than when I was drinking. It's the kind of discomfort that makes me want to unzip my flesh like a scuba suit, and step out of myself.

Long repressed emotions start bubbling up, with anger leading the charge. I'm no stranger to insane, sometimes violent thoughts, but now these are pure and potent, not diluted by alcohol. With the anger comes adrenaline, which for me, is like a real drug. It gives me a jolt of surging energy, and a sense of power. But unfortunately, it's always followed by an emotional hangover, which feels so similar to the ones I experienced hundreds of times in the mornings, after a night of heavy drinking. I begin to experience panic attacks, which I can best describe as, the feeling that you'd get visiting the zoo, if suddenly the cages disappear, and there's nothing between you and the vicious, wild animals. My insomnia returns in full force. When I *am* able to sleep, I often have vivid drinking dreams, from which I awaken, relieved to still be sober.

A way-too-happy guy at a meeting walks up to me. He gets in my face.

"You're new, aren't you, friend? How you doing?"

"Not too great. When's this shit start working?"

"Patience, son, around here we call it Slow-briety."

I think fuck you, but I say thanks. I hate all these sayings. They're everywhere; on the walls of meetings, coffee cups, car fenders, tee-shirts. Everyone spews these sayings like they're brainwashed robots. This spiritual bombardment is really getting to me. I need a break.

On cue, my sister Amy invites me to spend Thanksgiving with the family. I take my first trip back to Chicago as a sober guy, expecting to be greeted as a conquering hero. My expectations are not realized, as my three sisters seem uneasy with, and suspicious of, their new and improved brother. Of course they are; having lived through decades of me as a drunken tornado blowing through their lives, why should they automatically buy into the idea that I am now a changed man, someone to be trusted and respected?

My main source of relief and comfort in Chicago comes from Amy's daughter, my nine-month-old niece, Lexie. When I can't sleep in the middle of the night, I tiptoe into the nursery, and find that Lexie is always awake, too. I gently pick her up out of her crib, and we rock back and forth together. We gaze into each other's eyes for the longest time. A powerful bond is formed.

41

LAUGH RIOT

Back in L.A. again, I feel disoriented. It's always been desta-bilizing for me to bounce from one situation to another. I don't do well with change. I have a need for my surround-ings, and everything in them, to remain exactly as they are. I remember once completely losing my mind when I discovered that the spoons had been moved to forks drawer. But at the same time, returning to meetings, I'm struck by the fact that I drank every single day for the last sixteen years (with an involuntary, eight month hiatus in the loony bin), and for the last ninety days, I haven't had a single drink, and haven't really craved one. The most powerful compulsion I ever experienced, the thing that owned me, is now magically taken away. It's unbelievable. How did this happen? As much as I'd like to take full credit, I have a feeling it was not entirely my doing.

And then coincidences keep occurring, over and over. Parking spaces that have always been taken, are now free.

Residual checks from long forgotten shows appear in my mailbox when I need them most. I keep running into people from the meetings in the strangest places. I even hear a guy sharing, at a group level, about his obsession with feet. And I keep wondering what kept me alive while I was driving drunk out of my mind, for years.

Now that getting wasted no longer completely dominates my consciousness, images of female feet keep popping up in my head, like a Whac-a-Mole game. Not remotely ready to be with a real woman, I remember the movie I saw with mom, *Lolita,* and the gorgeous foot dominating the screen. I rent the movie week after week, reliving my introduction to the world of sex. I'm aware that, over time, purchasing the tape would be a lot cheaper than renting, but in my mind, purchasing would mean I have a problem.

I attend a speaker meeting, and the woman speaking, Claire, is hysterically funny. I laugh, and it feels so foreign. I realize I haven't laughed at all for many months. There hasn't been a hell of a lot to laugh about. Claire's story is compelling, and I identify with her in so many ways, even though we don't share the same gender, generation, background or ethnicity. More than anything, listening to Claire, I forget myself. It seems that alcoholism, and the recovery from it, transcend all demographics. The fact that my sponsor Stephan is gay and I am not never matters in the slightest.

I am invited to speak at a meeting—a large meeting, with over one hundred people in attendance. I desperately do not want to do this, but Stephan tells me I have no choice, that we always accept an AA request. On the day I am to speak, gazing out at the sea of alcoholic faces, my breathing becomes shallow. I have chosen a black shirt to wear, thinking it would be best at hiding the perspiration. I was wrong, my shirt is visibly drenched.

As I wait to be introduced, I am visited by my past, in the form of flashbacks (in Hebrew). I take to the podium, manage to get out a couple sentences, and then I faint dead away. The next thing I remember, I'm in Stephan's car. I'm mortified, completely filled with shame. I tell Stephan there's no way I can show my face at meetings anymore. He replies, "Fine, how do you want the mortician to dress you at your funeral?" I guess that black shirt would be appropriate. After a few days, I slink back to meetings.

4 2

MINGO THE MERCILESS

I haven't worked in a long time, and I've almost run out of my dad's possessions to sell. I have one item left, something I hoped I would never have to part with—an enormous plate adorned with paintings of bulls and bullfighters. It was my dad's prized possession. Mom bought it for him in Spain, as a wedding present. In my family, it's always been referred to as "The Picasso Plate." If it is indeed a Picasso, it's worth a fortune. Rather than find a job, I take the plate to an auction house to have it appraised. It turns out *not* to be a Picasso, but was painted at Picasso's school. I decide to sell it anyway. It kills me to sell it, especially for a fraction of what I hoped it was worth, but I'm in dire straits, and apparently unwilling to work for a living.

I go through the proceeds from the sale of the faux-Picasso quickly, and I'm finally faced with the stark reality that I have to get a real job, *now*. I hate to admit that I really don't know how find employment. I hear an elder at a men's stag meeting share about the best way to find a job, and that is to stand up at the men's stag meeting and announce that you need a job, then take whatever you're offered. And so I do, assuming that everyone knows who I think I am, and I will be offered a plum position in entertainment. The only job offer I get is from a one-eyed, Mexican, ex-con named Mingo, as his assistant furniture mover.

On the furniture moving job, Mingo will only refer to me as "Newcomer," never by my actual name. It's tough, exhausting work, and Mingo is a merciless tyrant. I complain to Stephan.

"Mingo treats me like a fucking slave. I shouldn't have to be doing shit work like this, in my thirties, with my background: top colleges, a member of the Directors *and* Writers Guilds, from a good family."

Stephan laughs at that last one. I concede.

"Okay, maybe not such a good family. But this job is nothing but a total humiliation."

Stephan responds.

"You sound like an asshole. Alcohol is the great equalizer, and AA is a place where lawyers go to plumbers to learn how to live."

I don't have a response for that. Stephan continues.

"And you're confusing humiliation with humility. Humiliation is when a hot girl comes to your room to fuck, and she finds you covered in your own puke."

I groan at the memory. Maybe I shouldn't have told Stephan about that.

"Humility is not thinking less of yourself, it's thinking of yourself less."

One thing I'm discovering is that I can't really trust my ability to clearly see my own reality. So often, I have some sort of encounter, usually unpleasant, and later report it to Stephan. I say to him, "This is what happened." And he says to me, "No, *this* is what happened." I am coming from a place of irrational emotion. Stephan is coming from a place of rational objectivity, and his perspective is almost always more accurate. This leads me to the revelation that sobriety is something I simply cannot do alone. It has to be a *we* deal. As much as I naturally tend to isolate, I can't afford to do it on a regular basis. If I rely exclusively on my own thinking, I am doomed.

43
BEAVER'S MOM

A couple months into the job as Mingo's assistant furniture mover, out of nowhere, I get an incredible job offer. I am asked to direct an episode of the sitcom, *The New Leave it to Beaver.* The show has the original cast of characters intact—all the actors who played...Beaver, Wally, Lumpy, Eddie Haskell, and quintessential mom, June Cleaver. Stephan says this opportunity materialized as a result of my willingness to do the job with Mingo. I don't see the connection, but my current vision is clouded with terror—this is a gig I think I could have aced when I was drinking. But now, as a not-too-tightly-wrapped, quivering jellyfish, there's no way I can walk onto a set and command a cast and crew.

Stephan somehow convinces me to at least show up for the first day of shooting, which turns out to be one of the worst days of my life. It starts out well, as I walk onto the set, and behold the perfectly recreated home of the Cleaver family, the family I so wanted to be a part of as a child. I can't believe I'm here. But as the work commences, in front of everyone on the set, I become a babbling idiot, with the shakes, and terrible case of dry mouth. I'm certain that they can all see the fear shooting out of my eyes. I am exposed as a talentless and pitiful fraud. At the end of the day, I go to the producer's office. He looks at me, sees how distraught I am.

"Rough day?"

"The roughest. Listen, I—I really think you should fire me. I don't know what the fuck I'm doing out there."

"Hey, give yourself a break. All first-time directors go through this."

"Not like *this*. You gotta fire me."

"You can quit, but I'm not going to fire you. This is the kind of thing that can really mess up your career."

"My career?" I laugh weakly.

"Why don't you just go home, relax, have a few beers, and think about it."

What I think about at home that night is that I should definitely start drinking again. There's no reason not to. I have just proved that sobriety does not work for someone like me. I notice the cast and crew phone list on my desk. I peruse the list, and am drawn to a particular name, Barbara Billingsley, who plays Beaver's mom, June Cleaver. I dial her number. Barbara answers, she sounds just like her. I identify myself and I get to the point, not wanting to waste her valuable time.

"I just want you know I won't be returning to the show. I'm obviously not really up to it, but it was such a tremendous honor meeting you, and working with you."

By this point, I'm beside myself, blubbering.

"When I was little, I wanted you to be my mom," I confess.

"That's nice, dear, but let's get a few things straight. You're not the first director I've had to coddle. You were just fine today. You *will* be returning to the set tomorrow, and the filming will go splendidly from here on out. All you have to do is trust me, get some sleep, and pray."

In between sniffles, I hear myself say, "Thank you, Mrs. Cleaver."

I follow Barbara's directions, and wake up the next morning with an almost total absence of anxiety. It's magic. It's spooky. It's real. I can't possibly understand what's happening. I spend all that day and the rest of the week's shoot in a kind of state of grace. I know what I'm doing. I act with calm and confidence. I say the right things to the actors and the crew. My mouth is no longer dry. I've never experienced anything like this. And, I don't drink. I will go on to direct many episodes of *Beaver*, but none are quite as magical.

4 4

STEPPING UP

Stephan is sick of hearing my lame excuses for not working the twelve steps of Alcoholics Anonymous. He informs me that he won't talk to me anymore until I begin this essential part of the program. Since Stephan is really the *only* person I speak with, I finally get down to business.

The first few steps are about finding a higher power. This is challenging for me; I can never forget the trauma of my bar mitzvah, where, if at *anytime* in my life, I figured God would have been present. He wasn't, or if he was, he didn't lift a finger to help me. The Jewish God let me down. Stephan points out that AA has nothing to do with religion, it's a *spiritual* program. Still, for me, the idea of a higher power is daunting, a heavy lift.

The middle steps deal with inventory and making amends; I write a lengthy "grudge list" containing everyone I've ever resented and why, and then I attempt to find *my* part in all my resentments. For me, this is a revolutionary concept; all my life I've never taken responsibility for my actions, always blaming everyone else. Now, to force myself to look honestly at where I was at fault, has a profound impact on my thinking, and therefore, my actions. For alcoholics, resentment is considered the number one offender. More sober alcoholics go back to drinking behind resentment than anything else.

Next, I read this inventory to my sponsor. It is excruciating to have to reveal myself and my secrets…most of which, I was planning to go to the grave with. When I get to my most embarrassing, shameful, awful secrets, Stephan doesn't seem at all scandalized. In fact, he shares some of *his* most horrendous secrets, which makes me feel like not such a monster. Slowly, my sense of terminal uniqueness is dissolving.

For the amends steps, I make a list of everyone I've harmed, then I go to them and offer my sincere apologies. It's difficult to face the people I've hurt, but it's what has to be done. One particularly memorable amends is with my step-father, Seymour. I balk at the idea of apologizing to him because he had hurt me so profoundly, but when pressed, I have to admit that I did my share of harm to him.

At a family holiday dinner in Chicago, I spot Seymour, now a much older man. He avoids me throughout the evening, but eventually, I find him alone in a room. I enter and close the door. I approach him, face to face. There is real terror in his eyes. He must think I'm going to kill him. The truth is I'd love to rip his throat out, but I simply say, "Seymour, I apologize for anything I ever did to harm you…and you might want to change your pants."

The final step is about carrying the message, being of service, helping people. And service isn't extended exclusively to other alcoholics. My aunt Jody has moved to L.A., she is very sick, and I visit her frequently, bring groceries, and just sit with her. I'm happy to do this, I love my aunt, but this is also a kind of living amends to my mom. I'm reminded over and over that the steps are not a one-time deal, but a lifelong process. On this initial tour, I gain some real clarity, including my newfound belief that all the shit that happened to me in my childhood did *not* cause my alcoholism. I believe I was born with the affliction, but what occurred in my childhood definitely *did* create a need for relief.

The American Medical Association has determined that Alcoholism is a disease. This means that alcoholics are sick people, not bad people. It's not a moral issue. This information is helpful to alcoholics, not as an excuse for their behavior, but as something that might keep them from being so hard on themselves, which is a common trait.

I have heard alcoholism called a "family disease." The alcoholic's illness has a kind of ripple effect on the members of their family, who become spiritually ill themselves. I now see that clearly in my effect on my sisters and mom, and in my dad's effect on me.

45
HP

My sobriety is progressing, but I continue to struggle with the idea of a higher power. I was raised, like so many boys, to believe that being a man meant a "John Wayne" kind of man—tough and strong and independent, who doesn't express his emotions or cry or ask for help, even if he clearly needs help. Even as a child, years before my bar mitzvah, the idea of God was troubling to me. At Sunday school, the old testament stories I heard made me think that God was an angry, punishing, frightening figure. The story that really got to me was the one about God telling Abraham to kill his son Isaac, and then when Abraham is about to do that, God basically says, "Just kidding!"

When I run this by Stephan, he tells me again that AA is all about the spiritual, not the religious, that I am free to choose whatever higher power I want, and call him or her by any name that works for me. He recommends that I just take the action of praying every day and see what happens. I don't even need to mean it. At worst, I might become a little less frazzled.

The eleventh step says, "Sought through prayer and meditation to improve our conscious contact with God, as we understood him." It's about *seeking*, not necessarily finding. The journey is what really matters, more than the destination. My higher power can be *anything* greater and more powerful than me. Over the years, my concept of a higher power evolves as I evolve. My initial higher power is Chicago Bulls superstar, Michael Jordan. I'm forgetting that the higher power doesn't have to be an individual, or a deity. If you're religious, you might have a higher power you're comfortable with already. Many people choose the ocean or nature. Others determine that the AA members themselves are their higher power—God as in Group Of Drunks. The only hard and fast rule is that your higher power should not be you.

I start to try to pray. I soon ditch Jordan, thinking I need something more personal and less defined. I start to just pray to the universe, hoping God will find me. In the beginning, I feel ridiculous, even embarrassed; I pray with my bedroom door closed, even though I live alone. It doesn't feel like I'm praying to anyone or anything. I make no connection at all. I go back to wanting a clear definition or even a visual of God, but that seems to be way beyond the capabilities of my mind. I hear so many people at meetings say that a relationship with a higher power is absolutely essential to their sobriety. I become terrified that I'm not going to be able to stay sober without a higher power. And for me, at this point, to drink is to die.

A couple months into my fruitless prayer ritual, a woman who knows I got sober asks me to talk to her younger brother who is having serious problems with drugs and alcohol. I can't imagine how I can help him, but I meet with her brother, Lorenzo, a nice kid in his teens, who isn't particularly receptive.

One distinction between religion and AA's spiritual approach is that AA is about "attraction rather than promotion." There is to be no recruiting, just the sharing of one's experience with another. So I share my experience with Lorenzo, and in the midst of our conversation, I hear myself talking about a higher power. It's coming from me, but I don't know how it got there. It seems that I have been infiltrated. I feel like a ventriloquist's dummy. But, what I am saying to Lorenzo is real, it comes from a place deep inside. After a couple hours, I give Lorenzo my phone number and we part ways. I never see or hear from Lorenzo again, but I walk away from our encounter with a flickering sense of God-consciousness, and some kind of higher power—one that I don't understand, and don't need to understand, in order to have in my life.

Every morning, I wake up with a head full of noise, screamingly negative noise; loud and insistent messages of fear, resentment, and doom. It's like my mind has become a prosecuting attorney, building a case for how hopeless I am. It waits all night, while I sleep, and the moment I open my eyes, it pounces on me.

Hoping to counter and quiet the daily bombardment of noise, I decide that I am going to try and practice meditation. The program provides so much personal freedom in so many areas: choosing a sponsor, determining a higher power, finding your own way to pray and meditate. Everything is suggested, never demanded. Although it *is* pointed out to me, if one jumps out of an airplane, it is *suggested* that you use a parachute.

I begin my quest to find the best way to meditate; I seek out a number of meditators who share their techniques and experience. I attend meditation classes. I read books on meditation. All of this research is valuable, but at some point, I realize that I am continuing my research in order to avoid actually meditating.

I finally get down to it; I meditate the moment I awaken in order to get the jump on the noise. My practice consists of different elements from the various subjects in my research. Basically, I get comfortable, close my eyes, repeat a short phrase, a kind of mantra, and I pay close attention to my breathing. It's difficult at first; I can't sit still, I'm distracted, I feel weird about it. But, it comes, with practice. Almost every time I meditate, the first thing I experience is the noise itself. It's like being in a space capsule, watching as meteors and space junk hurtle past. And it passes. After it does, I find this act of seeking to be deeply relaxing and comforting, a practice I emerge from refreshed and in a relatively positive frame of mind. To my surprise, meditation becomes a pleasant and restorative ritual I never go a day without.

Over time, a relationship with a higher power provides tangible benefits; one is that I find myself depending much less on other people. This dependence has always involved me placing unfair expectations and demands on others, basically insisting that they are responsible for me, and have to take care of me. This has, understandably, destroyed relationships and driven people away. Since I have become much less dependent on others, I experience a real improvement in the quality of my relationships.

Stephan tells me that "want" is at the core of my and most people's unhappiness in life. He suggests that wanting things from people causes expectations, and invariably, disappointment and resentment. Not wanting things from others, or not wanting them to be the way I want them to be, is almost as impossible as not thinking, as Stephan had recommended to me earlier. The key, I'm told, is acceptance, which is not something I'm naturally good at. So, like with everything else on this path, I have to consciously practice.

46
ROAD WARRIOR

My spiritual life is improving every day, but I'm *definitely* not up for sainthood. Among my still-existing demons, one stands out: for years, including in sobriety, I indulge in road rage, with a habit of chasing down cars when they've cut me off in traffic.

Recently, a car cut me off and almost caused me to have an accident. Instantly shot through with fear and adrenaline, I take off in my car, and begin to chase down the offending vehicle. Fueled by a delicious sense of menacing power, I weave crazily through traffic, shaking my fist, and pretending to yell. The driver of the car speeds up to get away. I follow the car for blocks. It finally has to stop at a red light. I screech up right behind it, close enough to read the sticker on the car's rear window, "Proud Parent of a Child at Temple Israel Day School." Oh, Jesus, I suddenly feel terrible.

I come to my senses. I need to make an immediate amends, so when the light turns green, I chase after the car again. At another red light, I pull side by side with the car, and signal to the woman at the wheel (with her young son in the backseat) to roll down her window, so I can apologize. She glances over, the look of terror and disgust she gives me before zooming away is chilling, and fills me with deep remorse.

I used to think that this sort of crazed behavior, my wildly exaggerated reaction to feeling fear, was automatic, that I have no choice. If nothing else, sobriety has given me choice: I can choose to drink or not, I can choose to terrorize motorists or not. Before I got sober, I could not choose not to drink, and once I took a drink, I could not choose how much I would drink, or what kind of reckless insanity I would engage in next. Now, I have to be aware that I always have a window, however brief, to choose. When I first got sober, like many fellow alcoholics, I expected to be immediately restored to emotional health, after decades of the drinking life, but the reality is that it takes many years to recover. As that guy at the meeting said, it really is "Slow-briety."

AA's second step, "Came to believe that a power greater than ourselves could restore us to sanity", suggests that I am, and probably will always be, somewhat insane. And when I am, I know it doesn't need to be a permanent, ongoing condition. I am capable of insane thinking and insane actions, but for a few years now, with the occasional lapse, I've mostly been able to keep my insanity largely between my ears, and not spilling out into the world.

Since I was a little kid, bouncing off the walls, I've occupied the extremes of any spectrum, sometimes simultaneously. I came to see myself as the piece of shit the world revolves around. I am now trying to find the gray area in life, a happy medium, the operative word being happy.

47
THE BIG HOUSE

As part of AA's hospital and institution outreach, panels of members go to visit with and speak to people who can't get to meetings. I am taken to a liver ward in a hospital, where there are rows of people in beds, suffering from liver disease. Many of them are yellow in color, with stomachs protruding out in a seemingly impossible way. It's disturbing to think that this is where my drinking was taking me. Almost all of them are alcoholics. I go bed to bed, talking with the patients. I simply can't believe how many of them insist that they have no problem with alcohol. The power of denial is truly extraordinary.

I am asked to speak at a prison, where the vast majority of the inmates' crimes were alcohol or drug-related. A couple of sober pals and I enter a large, windowless room in the prison. It's a scary scene—dozens of stone-faced, tough-looking inmates, many in hairnets, and—in my imagination—with shivs hidden in their clothing. A couple of sleepy armed guards lean against the walls. When it's my time to speak, I stand and look out at the disinterested, unwelcoming crowd. I register the fear I feel, and I proceed to speak honestly and from the heart. I'm shaky, but I do not faint. There is zero reaction to my talk, except for a few yawns. I am aware that there might be a guy or two who is interested or relates, but it's not safe for them to show that in this environment. I can only hope that we've had an impact, or maybe just planted a seed. When I'm done speaking, I take a seat. The clank of the prison gate closing behind me is a sweet, sweet sound. Years later, I will have my own panel with four or five different speakers each month who join me on visits to prisons and institutions.

Around that time, my grandmother Nonnie passes away, at ninety-three. I am asked to speak at her funeral. When I do, I discover that I have a total absence of fear. It occurs to me later that I was speaking not about myself, but about someone else, entirely.

48
FRIEND OF BILL

Speaking at the prison and at Nonnie's funeral gives my confidence the kind of boost that allows me to seriously consider the next job offer I receive; a Romanian friend from film school, Doro, needs a feature-length script written about the Ceausescu regime (as far from *Beaver* as you get). Doro sells me on the job, leaving the worst for last—the screenplay has to be written *in Romania,* because the writer has to see the places he's writing about. Wanting an "out," I discuss it with Stephan, who, of course, thinks it's a "splendid idea… an adventure! That's why you got sober, to have adventures."

Doro meets me at the Bucharest airport, and drives to the outskirts of the city, finally stopping at an ancient, bullet-ridden tower. He looks up at the structure.

"This is home for you next few months."

"You're shitting me," I say, in disbelief.

"Doro does not shit."

My "home" is a tiny, cell-like chamber, up countless stairs, at the very top of the tower. It's the time before the internet. There's no phone, no hot water, and I soon discover, no AA meetings in all of Romania. An adventure indeed. I've been attending meetings almost every day for a couple of years now, and I have come to depend on regular contact with other sober folks. I hope this doesn't become a problem.

It becomes a problem. After a couple months in the tower, the screenwriting is going well, but the isolation is taking a real toll on me. I feel like a prisoner. The producers are friendly guys who see I'm having a rough time, but they can't seem to understand that taking me to discos, and enticing me with drinks isn't going to get them a better script.

I'm in touch frequently with my higher power, but I start to feel almost desperate for contact with fellow alcoholics. I remember a code phrase that recovering people use to determine if someone else is sober: "Are you a 'Friend of Bill?'" (referring to Bill Wilson, AA's founder). Extremely eager to find a member of my new tribe, I start hanging around the production office, listening for any sober buzz words. I hear a guy whose English isn't terrible, saying the word "meeting" a bunch of times. I wait for the right moment, then I corner him.

"Are you a friend of Bill?"

"Yes, I am friend of Bill."

I'm overjoyed. I actually hug the stranger. I pour my heart out to him.

"Man, am I glad to see you! I've been stuck in that fucking tower forever. No meetings, no people, no nothing. They should tell you there are no meetings in this fucking country. I have got so much fucking fear shooting through me, and insecurity, and doubt, and I'm lonely as fuck."

The Romanian guy, who has been staring at me in confusion during my outpouring, now looks at something over my shoulder. He points.

"There is Bill."

The Bill he points to is a carpenter, carrying planks of wood. I'm disappointed my new friend isn't a sober dude, and I doubt Bill is either, but, oddly, I feel greatly relieved after sharing my pain, even a small amount of it.

I travel to the Yucatan Peninsula in Mexico to make a documentary about the Mayan ruins there. The documentary is never completed, but I have a powerful experience. Whenever I'm in another country or city, I always try to find out where there are AA meetings. Finding a meeting here in the Yucatan is a long shot, but I ask the guy at the hotel desk if he knows of any AA meetings on Sunday, my only free day. He thinks about it, says he'll get back to me later.

The next day, he gives me an address and a time. I'm surprised and thankful. I attend the meeting. Seven or eight locals sit in a circle. They couldn't be more friendly and welcoming. When everyone shares, I don't know what they're saying, and they don't know what I'm saying, but we understand one another. After the meeting, I say to the guy with the best English, "See you next Sunday." He looks at me quizzically. I repeat what I said. He says there's no meeting next Sunday. I don't understand. He tells me that the sober folks in town heard of a foreigner who needed a meeting, so they all came and created one. I'm amazed.

This experience, more than anything I can think of, explains what Alcoholics Anonymous is all about.

49
LEND YOU MY EAR

A while after my return from the Yucatan, a young guy with a few days of sobriety, Pedro, asks me to be his sponsor. I'm nervous and reluctant, I've never sponsored anyone before. I consult with Stephan.

"This new guy, Pedro, asked me to be his sponsor."

"That's terrific. Congratulations."

"I don't know…"

"What's not to know? This is the best thing that could happen to you. It'll be great."

"Right, another '*adventure*,'" I say sarcastically.

"Oh, you're gonna shit on the idea without even experiencing it? That kind of thinking makes your world pretty fucking small…and boring. Besides, sponsoring isn't that difficult. All you have to do is listen…and share your experience, strength and hope…and guide him through the steps…and women dig guys who sponsor."

I become Pedro's sponsor. We talk frequently. I do a lot of listening. When I'm speaking with Pedro, I am focused on Pedro, and I have the experience once again of losing myself. It's a state of grace; I feel no self-consciousness, the right words come effortlessly. Sometimes, I feel like I'm channeling. And I get to see and feel Pedro making real strides in his comfort and confidence. This is what it's like to not be "useless."

At a meeting one day, I hear a guy sharing. The voice is familiar. He says he's new to sobriety, and that he's certain he can't be helped. The face is familiar. Then, it hits me. In yet another crazy coincidence, I am listening to Jamie, who got kicked out of boarding school when he got caught hiding *my* booze in *his* locker. I never admitted it was mine. I approach Jamie after the meeting. and insist that he *can* be helped, by me. I tell him, "I've got twenty years of guilt to work off. I'm your sponsor." Then I shake Jamie's hand and make him agree to what Stephan made me agree to, when we first met, "We do not drink, we do not use, one day at a time, *no matter what.*"

I wind up sponsoring Brandon, a great guy who is in a famous rock band. He tours all over the world, and calls me from faraway places. Brandon tells me stories of his glamorous but far from happy life. I listen, then suggest potential solutions, which often include stories of my own experiences.

Brandon has everything a guy could ever want; fame, wealth, a mansion, expensive cars, hot and cold running women, yet he's plagued by insecurity, loneliness, and fear. It's difficult for me to understand. I had always assumed that having all that "stuff" would make anyone completely happy, and impervious to life's bumps and bruises. Brandon's situation is illuminating to me, and makes me embrace the idea the old-timers always stress; if you are seeking maximum comfort and serenity in your life, it is indeed an "Inside Job."

Sometimes, I think that what AA boils down to is storytelling. Stories are told in the big book of Alcoholics Anonymous. Stories are told by speakers in meetings. And stories are told when an alcoholic shares at a meeting. Perhaps most importantly, stories are shared, one alcoholic to another, in sponsor-sponsee relationships. Often these stories are entertaining as well as informative. They encourage not only identification, connection, and the sense that one is not alone, but also, deflection. It is a fact that alcoholics are extremely self-involved. Self-obsessed fear is at the route of our problems. When one alcoholic talks to another, listens, and tells stories, the teller of the story is focused on the listener, not so much on himself, and the listener is paying attention to the teller's story, so his self-obsession is interrupted. Even a momentary deflection of an alcoholic from himself or herself is an enormous relief.

50

PRANKSTER

I start a monthly meeting at my apartment for the guys I sponsor. A regular attendee of this meeting is Angus, a brilliantly funny, exceedingly edgy behemoth. The meeting is often followed by a session of phone pranking, with Angus holding court.

The years before Caller ID were a glorious time for phone pranksters, and Angus is in a class by himself. These post-meeting sessions take on a ritualistic quality; we gather in my bedroom, everyone always in the same seats. I dim the lights, and distribute pillows for the guys to laugh into. Angus activates the speaker phone, then flips through the Yellow Pages or my personal phone book, looking for victims. Angus waits for the rest of us to beg him to begin, then launches into his hilarious and often mean-spirited phone pranks. He calls a variety of targets; a bakery, saying he wants a wedding cake, but that he's a dwarf, and needs the figurines cut off at the knees… a hardware store, talking an employee into breaking into a stolen safe… a sign maker who Angus convinces to make truly offensive signs for sketchy organizations. Angus phones barbershops, law offices, tattoo parlors, doctors, banks, sororities, actors (famous and not), members of AA, and a number of my own relatives.

Listening to Angus on the phone, the rest of us laugh until we're on the floor, gasping for breath. This pranking is obviously quite juvenile, and reminds me of something I heard at a meeting—"The emotional development of an alcoholic stops at the age he starts drinking." Sobriety encourages maturity, but a part of me still subscribes to the words of my favorite singer/songwriter, Elvis Costello, "So what if this is a man's world, I want to be a kid again about it." Eventually, as entertaining as the pranking is, something feels wrong about what we're doing, and I call an end to the post-meeting phone pranks, which are really not in keeping with what we're trying to accomplish in meetings. Angus is furious with me. I have robbed him of his main stage, and his adoring audience, the only love he experiences.

Angus is a true artist, but he's also deeply troubled, and he lives to provoke. People at the meetings are scared of him. They often worriedly ask me if Angus is going to hurt them. A short time after the dissolution of the pranking, I'm riding shotgun in Angus's truck. He starts to drive dangerously. I ask him to knock it off. He ignores me, and drives faster. I scream at him, but he just grins like a lunatic. I finally get out of the truck, while it's moving, and tumble to the curb. Angus drives up on the sidewalk, gets out of his truck, and lifts me up against a wall, his hands around my throat. I can't breath. I start to black out. I truly think I'm going to die. Angus finally lets go of me, and returns to his truck, without a word. I walk home, and by the time I get back, there are a number of phone messages from Angus, crying and apologizing.

As a sponsor, I am *not* a trained therapist. I have experience with alcoholism and sobriety, and I can be helpful with those issues. Occasionally, it becomes clear to me that someone I'm sponsoring may be in need of more help than AA and I can provide. When that occurs, I recommend that they seek outside or professional help. That kind of recommendation is often not welcome. Some sober guys want to believe that AA is a panacea, that it alone will solve *all* of their problems. That simply isn't the case.

I sit down with Angus and tell him that even though I'm not completely comfortable spending time with someone who might kill me, I will continue to be his sponsor, but only if he seeks professional help, in addition to AA. Angus refuses; he is profoundly attached to his illness, he depends on it for his identity. He allows his craziness to define him. We hug and part company. I love Angus, and I wish him well. And I miss him.

I am asked to serve as an Ala-tot sponsor—presiding over a group of seven to twelve-year-olds whose families are impacted by alcoholism. I feel closer to these kids than the adults at the meetings I attend. Hearing them talk openly and honestly about their parents' alcoholism and how it affects them is deeply moving, and makes me wish I had access to something like this when I was a kid.

Sponsoring, whether it ends well or not, is a godsend. It allows me the opportunity to experience, on a regular basis, not only the feeling of usefulness, but the exquisite relief of what is known in AA literature as, "Freedom from the bondage of self."

51
HIGH WIRE

When I first got sober, I was afraid that life was going to be dull and boring, but a number of years into sobriety, it's anything but. I used to drink to take the edge off, now there's *only* edge. It feels like a high wire act, without a net or any kind of buffer. Life comes straight at me, and I no longer hide or flee. I take it on. I feel everything. I'm totally alive. I hardly ever experience the obsession to drink or use, but I have to stay vigilant; it's easy to forget this is a life-and-death deal. I've attended too many funerals of sober friends who started drinking again.

I am enjoying a kind of reincarnation. Slowly, buried parts of me become unearthed and reemerge: a long dormant sense of humor, creativity, the love of physical activity. And entirely new parts appear; social comfort, acceptance, faith, an emergence from the shadows.

Over time, I become more visible at the meetings, I allow myself to be known, and my fellow drunks seem to like me.

They elect me secretary of a large meeting where I am responsible for running the meeting, and for choosing speakers. I travel all over L.A., looking for speakers at meetings I've never been to. I have the secretary commitment for one year. It's a position of real responsibility—never my strong suit. And it forces me to look at my control issues. At first, I feel naked and vulnerable. Everyone at the meeting has access to me, which often comes in the form of complaints: I'm getting too many gay speakers, not enough gay speakers, too many old-timers, not enough old-timers, etc. It's aggravating, but I come to enjoy the interactions, and I finish my term with, for the first time in a while, a feeling of real accomplishment.

From the age of sixteen, when I was diagnosed with Manic Depression (aka Bipolar Disorder), until thirty, when I got sober, I swung like a yo-yo, from depression to mania. Lithium was prescribed for me in the bin, but I never took it on a regular basis. Even if I had, it's doubtful it would have been effective, with all of the drugs and alcohol I was consuming, at the time. Once I got clean and sober, my illness was finally able to be treated by medical specialists. For years now, manic depression has not been an issue for me.

There are those in AA who espouse what I consider to be a very dangerous message—that if the sober alcoholic takes anything at all that affects him from the neck up (including non-addictive anti-depressants), he is *not* sober. The hardliners who hold to this belief are extremely vocal, and in my opinion, they are coming from a place of fear and hysteria, almost never from actual, personal experience. I have seen people in AA affected by terrible depression, who are bullied into *not* taking anti-depressants, and in end, commit suicide. I was, for a long time, silent about my own experience, and cowed by the hardliners. But with some solid sobriety under my belt, I am silent no more. I make a few enemies, but this is about principles, not personalities.

Looking back, it is now clear to me that my dad suffered horribly from manic depression (as well as alcoholism). If a solution was available at that time—and I don't know if there was one—he never sought it. My dad lived a sad and tortured life, and he did a great deal of harm to those of us who loved him. My rage toward him has been eating me alive my entire life. In the book *To Kill a Mockingbird*, Atticus Finch explains to his daughter, Scout, "You never really understand a person until you consider things from his point of view…until you climb into his skin and walk around in it." When I finally climb into my dad's skin, I discover a very familiar terrain, littered with terror, remorse, despair, loneliness, and utter powerlessness over alcohol. The only difference between dad and me is that I was fortunate to find a way out. Practicing the principles of sobriety has given me that way out, as well as a newfound compassion for my dad. I have found a place of forgiveness. Over twenty-five years after his death, I am finally able to mourn for my dad.

Sometimes, I wonder if my dad hadn't died, would he have gotten clean, and would we have enjoyed a great relationship; traveling to the bullfights in Spain together, winning boat races together, celebrating our victories with sparkling cider together, just being together. Those moments are never going to happen. They are, of course, fantasies, but thinking like this feels so much better than thinking about dad the way I have for years.

5 2

FINAL FRONTIER

As for my career, it's not remotely close to where I want it to be, but I am able to score an occasional writing or directing gig, and I show up and do a professional job. I run into my old English teacher and football coach, Mr. Mitchell. It turns out he is also a frustrated screenwriter, and we collaborate on a spec script called "Stone Age Cheerleaders," which garners lots of laughs, but, sadly, no income.

The most encouraging aspect of my life is that, in AA, I have become part of something. This makes it easier to be and feel a part of other things, like the human race. I am much less isolated, and find myself actually enjoying being around people. Life is on the upswing...except for romantic relationships, which remain a real challenge, the final frontier.

It's easy to date in AA; potential partners are right in front of me, every day. I don't have to go to bars and parties to meet them, or get fixed up by well-meaning but clueless friends. And these women are great-looking, interesting, charismatic, and have so much in common with me. But, they are alcoholics like me, and everything that comes with that.

I have a tendency to go along with other's agendas, and minimize my own, especially with women. I meet Diane at a meeting. She seems to be interested in me, so automatically I'm hers, regardless of whether or not I have a real interest in her. Diane is an attractive woman with a big personality, and a successful career. She is an actress on a long-running TV sitcom. I have to admit I'm dazzled by that. She makes big bucks, but according to her AA sponsor, I, as a man, have to court her, seemingly indefinitely.

Diane starts to direct her TV show, and becomes increasingly controlling. She begins to try to "direct" my life. The first time we have sex, Diane instructs me on how to make love, what I should do, where to place my hands, etc., ending with a stern warning, "There will be no anal sex." I respond, "But that's my specialty!" I'm kidding, but Diane is not amused. It's hard to take, especially from a woman with mediocre feet. I feel I've become just another part of her entourage, along with agent, manager, PR person, hair stylist, personal assistant—I am boyfriend, an appendage to wear on her arm.

Diane insists that I escort her to a star-studded benefit concert with Barbra Streisand top-lining. Diane never warns me that as we enter the theater, we will be walking past a row of reporters and photographers, many of whom holler out, "Diane, who's the man with you?" and "Who's the guy?" Diane doesn't answer. The photographers keep asking the question. Finally, I have enough of being invisible, and I blurt out, "My name is Yaphet Kotto" (an older black actor). The next day, a Hollywood trade paper reports that Diane is dating Yaphet Kotto. I am summarily fired from the job of boyfriend. Free at last.

I try the AA relationship route a few more times, but with the intense levels of drama and insanity (both parties), dating often feels like a heavyweight fight. Stephan recommends that I check out Al-Anon, another twelve-step program for people intimately involved with alcoholics. Al-Anon meetings are much like AA meetings, same steps, same lingo, with a different focus. Al-Anon proves helpful, especially with the concept of "detachment," and I eventually come to a conclusion—one alcoholic in a relationship is enough.

53
DWARVES

A couple I know want to fix me up with a woman they think is perfect for me. I'm not even going to discuss this with Stephan, I already know what he'll say—"bla, bla, bla, adventure!" With considerable trepidation, I finally agree to a blind date with a woman named Stacey, who turns out to be a pretty, sweet, non-alcoholic, red-haired Mormon. She's good company, we date for a while, and, as is so often the case with dating, I don't wind up seeing her feet for a quite a long time. When I finally do, I discover something I've never seen before—dwarf second toes. I don't react, at least externally. Rather, I continue to show up for what is becoming a real relationship.

Stacey is such a lovely woman, and I try so hard to ignore or accept the dwarves, but, in the end, I simply can't. The tiny toes loom larger and larger. After a good amount of inner turmoil, I decide to break up with Stacey, telling her it's because of religious differences. I feel like such a shallow asshole. I *am* a shallow asshole. I hate myself.

I begin working feverishly on my foot problem; I perform spiritual exercises, I see a therapist, I try to pray it away, I even get hypnotized. Nothing helps. I become distraught, and I inform Stephan I'm worried if I don't think of something fast, I might start drinking again. Stephan provides a little tough love.

"Your problem isn't drinking, it's thinking. Whenever you think, the only thing you think about is you, and you scare the shit out of yourself. The problem isn't what you think, it's *that* you think."

"The only way I can stop thinking is by having a lobotomy," I say in despair.

"That would do the trick, but it's a little extreme. You stop thinking by getting off your ass and start *doing*."

"Doing what?"

"*Anything*. Anything that keeps you from thinking about you. Anything is better than mind-fucking yourself all day long. You're trying too hard, kid, you're forcing it. Just trust the fucking process."

So I throw myself into action, sometimes constructive, sometimes mindless; cleaning my apartment, washing the car, doing laundry, playing tennis, jogging, biking, swimming, working out, writing, reading, alphabetizing my music, anything to keep from sitting and thinking.

Bill Wilson, the founder of AA, wrote, "The primary fact that we fail to recognize is our total inability to form a true partnership with another human being." The man knew his stuff, and I know that my issues with relationships aren't just about feet. I have always had a good deal of fear and confusion around women and sex. Drinking had effectively obliterated my fear, and allowed me to have a love life, but sober now, intimacy is excruciating; I almost pass out on dates, and I can't stand to have a woman sleep over.

And my issues aren't just about sex, either. They involve so many more factors; communication, honesty, trust, vulnerability. It's overwhelming. I've got to just try to let go, and trust the "fucking process."

5 4

SCENE OF THE CRIME

I turn my attention to a different kind of action, part of the process I'm supposed to be trusting. I go back to working the steps, and I start making more amends. When I was initially confronted with the extensive list of people I had harmed, and owed an amends to, I was afraid to face many of them, and I put off my amends for later. Now, it's later. I call, write, or meet with the remaining people on my list, even my mother (speaking to her photo), who I'm able to forgive for not being June Cleaver. My drinking had caused me to fall into disfavor with everyone in my family, who were either frightened of me, or for me. I am finally able to ease their minds, as well as my own.

Now, as I throw myself into more amends-making, I experience a real healing with my three sisters, and by extension, my nieces and nephews. Since I left home for school, I haven't seen that much of Jewel and Liza over the years, except on occasional vacations. Both of them have become successful women with wonderful families. None of my sisters suffer from alcoholism or bipolar illness; interesting, when you consider we all have the same (or almost the same) genes. Guess I was just lucky.

My sister Amy has been utterly obsessed with Disneyland since she was a child, so she starts to take regular trips out to L.A. with Lexie, now a seven-year-old force of nature, and they stay with me, at my place. Lexie is an extraordinary swimmer, and she and I spend endless hours together in the pool, even though it's not heated. We visit Disneyland, which Lexie calls "Dizzyland." I don't find this theme park to be the "Happiest Place on Earth", but I do find that I am the happiest guy around Lexie.

My oldest nephew, Liza's son, twelve-year-old David, calls from Chicago, and grills me.

"You're Jewish, right, Uncle Duffy?"

"Right."

"You're a writer, right?"

"Right."

"You were bar mitzvah, right?"

"Well…"

"Will you write my bar mitzvah speech?"

"No, I won't write your speech, but I *will* work on it with you."

And so we begin one of my favorite writing collaborations, ever. Over the course of a few months, David and I are in touch frequently by phone and email as we write and then fine tune his speech. When it's finished, it positively sings. David invites me to his bar mitzvah in Chicago, and insists that I *have* to attend.

In Chicago, as we park near the synagogue, I have a queasy feeling; it's the same place where I was bar mitzvah twenty-five years ago. We enter the main room, the old Frankenstein Center, where nothing at all has changed, it is *exactly* the same—the scene of the crime. At David's bar mitzvah, I sit next to Lexie. She tugs at my sleeve, and points to someone.

"Uncle Duffy, is that old man with the beanie part of our family?"

"It's called a yarmulke, and that's your great uncle, Ralph," I whisper.

"He doesn't look so great to me."

I laugh out loud, and am shushed by surrounding temple-goers.

When David performs his speech, he is superb. I'm like a stage mother, mouthing the words along with him. It's like I'm being bar mitzvah all over again, but this time, not a single mistake.

I phone Stephan after the bar mitzvah, to give him the glowing report. Stephan is astounded.

"You're telling me you had the time of your life in a *synagogue?*"

"Yes! The same exact same place where I got fucking destroyed when I was a kid."

"Interesting."

"My nephew aced every single note I gave him. He was perfect."

"No such thing."

"Fine, he was very, very, very good."

"You are aware that you didn't engineer this whole thing?"

"Thanks for pissing on my parade."

"You know what I mean."

"Right, I've read the book, too, 'Any success we may be having is more God's success than ours,' but don't *I* get a little credit?"

"A little…although I do think this was a big win for you."

David's bar mitzvah is indeed a profound, personal triumph, one that allows me to begin to finally let go of much of the ruinous fallout from my own bar mitzvah experience. It's been an unusually pleasant visit with the family, and I'm not looking forward to returning to the coast, where the main thing waiting for me is my ongoing struggle with work.

When I return to L.A., the last thing I want to do is face the reality of my career. I want to avoid. I want to escape. Alcoholics, like me, are great escapists. Most of us can get addicted to *anything*. Once we give up drinking and drugs, many addicts wind up finding a replacement addiction or obsession. This is referred to in meeting lingo as a "lateral move." Among the most common lateral moves are obsessions with food, shopping, sex, the internet, pornography and gambling. My own go-to obsession is sports on TV, and particularly Chicago sports teams. This goes back to childhood, and has only gotten stronger. I am the proud owner of NFL, NBA and NHL season passes, and I never miss an opportunity to escape, via a Bears, Bulls or Blackhawks game.

But, in the end, there's only so much sports a guy can watch, and I finally drag myself away from the TV screen, and return to the business of trying to breathe life into my livelihood.

55
STAN THE FAN

When I originally decided to be a film director, in my early twenties, it was all about ego and ambition. The longer I'm sober, the smaller my ego seems to be, and my ambition isn't nearly what it was. Hence, I no longer direct. I do continue to write, and although I've never felt more creative and less blocked, writing work is increasingly difficult to find. Once in a great while, I'm hired to adapt a book, or as a "script doctor." I also write "spec" scripts (for fun and for free), which are a joy, and meaningful to me, but at best, they wind up in development for years, before ultimately dying.

It is suggested to me that having a manager (in addition to an agent) might provide a real boost to my career. I am given a recommendation for a manager, a guy named Zach, who, after not showing up for a couple meetings, asks me if I have anything I'd like to write. I tell him I've been thinking of a script about an obsessive sports fan, and I go into great detail about the character and the story. Zach loves the idea, but he and I differ considerably on the tone; Zach thinks it should be extremely broad, almost cartoonish, while I want it to be more subtle, a blend of humor and drama. The main character is an addict, which might be a tough sell, but a *sports* addict may be viewed as commercial enough, and still allow me to explore the darker themes that are close to me. Zach and I can't agree. In the end, I just go off to write it, my way.

When I finish the screenplay, *Stan the Fan*, I'm very proud of it. It's my best work ever. I show it to Abe who loves it, and takes it to Paramount. The studio is seriously interested in buying and filming my script. I am ecstatic. I call Zach with the great news. His response is strange, to say the least.

"Oh, no," Zach says.

"What the hell do you mean, 'oh, no'? This is the best news I've ever told anyone."

"I, uh, I just sold my version of the script to Universal."

"*Your* version?! What the hell are you talking about?!" I shout in total disbelief.

"Listen, I can probably get you a few grand…"

"You disgusting piece of shit," I yell. And I slam down the phone.

I'm crushed. My own representative has stolen my idea and sold it. This ends Paramount's interest in my script, and makes it impossible for me to write at all. Addicts have an uncanny ability to find other addicts, and I discover later that Zach is a gambling addict. The meetings he had missed with me earlier were because he was at the horse track. The effect of Zach's betrayal is more than just monetary. Since childhood, I have had a serious inability to trust people, especially those who are supposed to be in my corner. In the past few years, I've worked on that, and made some real headway. Now, I'm back to square one.

When bad things happen to me, I have a long history of making them worse. As a child, occasionally my mom would slap me in the face, never that hard, but when she did, I would throw myself across the room, slam into a wall, collapse in a heap, and hope there was blood. Later in life, when I've been wronged, I've had the need to advertise the injuries, to exaggerate the damage, and to proclaim my victimhood. I've always done that in a self-destructive manner. Now, I'm hoping to break that pattern.

I talk to Stephan who helps me deal with my disappointment and feelings of betrayal, but he suggests that I also talk to a lawyer. Whenever I go to Stephan about matters in which he has no experience, he always recommends that I find someone with experience to talk to. "Experience is golden," Stephan says, "Opinions are like assholes, everyone has one, and they usually stink." He recommends a lawyer, who happens to be sober. The lawyer says I have good case, but that if I sue, I will probably wake up everyday at war, possibly for years. As much as I want to see Zach punished, I opt for peace. This decision is probably the right thing for me, but, as a revenge junkie, I'm never entirely comfortable with it.

I try to get back into the swing of things again, but in my early 40s, I feel *old*. I pitch story ideas to shockingly young execs who have never heard of Akira Kurosowa. My confidence starts to erode further, and I become terribly anxious again, eventually experiencing a full-blown panic attack while pitching a promising project to a roomful of studio execs. After that experience, I can't seem to get my ass out of bed to look for work. The bottom line; I'm capable of being miserable and rich, or happy and poor, what I don't do too well is miserable and poor.

Finally, things get so bad I can no longer make payments on the modest condo I purchased a few years earlier. I am foreclosed on. For the first time in years, I really think about drinking, but I am reminded by Stephan that drinking is no longer an option for me. It can only make things even worse. After more than ten years of sobriety, I find myself at a personal low point, or "no" point—no career, no relationship, no money, no home.

I trudge around town, looking for a cheap place to rent. In a haze, and reeling from the shame of my foreclosure, I find a decent building that I fail to realize is occupied almost exclusively by gay men, with just a few straight women. As I ride the elevators in this place, it's clear that my new neighbors assume that I am gay. Perhaps it's the people pleaser in me, or maybe the chameleon, but I don't correct their assumptions.

56
HER

One day, a woman who lives in the new building enters the elevator; a smashing, blue-eyed, brunette Brit in a tennis outfit that shows off her amazing legs. Do they lead to amazing feet? As we descend to the ground floor, I realize that she too assumes I'm gay. I try to disabuse her of that misconception by introducing myself in a particularly husky voice. She laughs at my ridiculousness, shakes hands, and says her name is Poppy. As she disappears into the parking garage, I blurt out as I mime swinging a racquet, "Hey, you know, we should rally sometime." "We may," Poppy teases. And we do. On the tennis court, I discover that Poppy is a single mom with a young daughter and a great backhand. She's not an alcoholic, and doesn't seem to care that I am.

We inch from tennis into dating, a very slow process—I haven't had much success with the accelerated approach. Aside from Poppy's looks, I'm so attracted to her warmth, optimism, intelligence, sense of humor, and infectious joie de vivre. What the fuck is she doing with *me?*

A central concept in AA is the idea of "Practicing the Principles" (honesty, forgiveness, service, acceptance, non-judgement, etc.). I have to consciously practice these principals because I'm not naturally good at them. I'm awed that Poppy seems to have had the principles installed at birth. We discuss resentment, my favorite pastime. When Poppy says she simply doesn't have resentments, I howl, "What the hell is the matter with you?" I mean that jokingly, but I kind of do resent the fact that she doesn't resent.

When we're together, I am surprised that I'm able to pay complete attention to her, and not to what I think she's thinking about me. The more attached I'm becoming to Poppy, the more a specific fear creeps into my mind—a fear about feet, Poppy's feet in particular. I haven't seen them yet, but what if they're horrible? Even if they are gnarly crab claws, I think I'll still want to be with her, but I do have a lingering doubt. I become afraid to see her feet, and I keep arranging the sort of dates where Poppy will have to wear shoes—tennis, hiking, dancing, even bowling.

Finally, as the weather warms up, I decide, enough of my bullshit; it's time to take the plunge, and I invite Poppy to a picnic on the beach. I have finally admitted to myself that I love this woman, and I am ninety-nine percent committed to continuing to love her, regardless of how monstrous her feet might be. On the beach, I hold my breath as Poppy ever so slowly removes her gym shoes. Her feet…are fine, they're nice, they're lovely. They're not perfect (one second toe is a tad too long, the fourth toes are semi-cashew-like, and the toenail polish could use a freshening), but they're lovely, and I love them, maybe because they're attached to *her*.

The only chink in the amour armor is that Poppy's six-year-old daughter, Char, seems to actively dislike me, and resents the time I spend with her mom. When I go to pick up Poppy for a date, Char answers the door with a hostile…

"*You* again!"

"Nice to see you too, Char. I'm here for your mom."

"She's not here," Char proclaims, crossing her arms.

At which point, I can only smile sheepishly at Poppy, who stands over Char's shoulder. But I think I understand how Char feels. I remember how awful it was when my mom introduced strange men into our lives, and how much I despised her dates. At least Char doesn't spit in my beverages…to my knowledge.

I don't allow Char's lack of enthusiasm to burst my bubble; I tell Stephan I can't believe how quickly my life has gone from misery to mirth. He tells me, "Your vision is limited, my friend. You've got to try to see the big picture. You've got to trust. There's a reason for everything. If you hadn't lost your home to foreclosure, you never would've met Dream Girl." Point taken.

57

WOLFE AT THE DOOR

As much as I'd like to continue to focus solely on matters of the heart, at this point, attention to my rocky career is required. An unexpected lifeline comes from my old pal, Abe, who is interested in producing a feature film about one of the most powerful and colorful figures in the music business, a mogul who I will call "Wolfe." Abe says that he thinks I would be the perfect person to write the screenplay, as Wolfe has a history of drug and alcohol abuse, and has recently gotten sober. I jump on the opportunity. I am tasked with writing a screen adaptation of a book about Wolfe, written by the great ghost writer, David Ritz, a wonderful guy who is exceptionally generous and supportive. Wolfe insists that I travel to New York City for a week (on his dime), to spend some time with him, and get to know one another.

Wolfe, a bull of a man in his mid-seventies, puts me up at a trendy hotel in Soho. On my first night there, I hear a soft knock at the door. I open it on one of the most beautiful woman I've ever seen, wearing a little too much make-up. I barely get the words out...

"Can I help you?"

The woman slides past me, into my hotel room.

"Wolfe sent me. I'm Jewel."

"That's my sister's name," I blurt out.

"How exciting."

Jewel shimmies out of her coat, revealing something scant underneath. I finally get it.

"Yes, well, Jewel, you are absolutely gorgeous, just a fantastic looking woman, but I—I'm in a relationship, and I can't really... God, why couldn't this have happened when I was single?"

Jewel reluctantly starts to put her coat back on.

"I understand, but Wolfe is not gonna be happy."

I hurriedly escort the escort to the door before I can change my mind.

"Wolfe will be fine, I'll tell him you gave me the best blowjob I've ever had."

"Oh, that's sweet. Thanks a bunch."

Jewel exits, and I close the door on the night of my life.

For one week, it's all Wolfe all the time; an enormously wealthy retiree, Wolfe guides me through the Village, regaling me with amazing tales from his wild and debauched life, which can be summed up as "sex, drugs and rock and roll, on steroids."

"I tell you that I banged the Pointer Sisters?" Wolfe boasts.

"Really?"

"All three of them."

"Wow," I exclaim, truly awed.

"Not bad, for a poor Jewish kid from Brooklyn, huh?"

"Very impressive."

"You a Yid?"

"I'm Jewish."

"Glad to hear it. Stay that way."

Wolfe is the hero of all of his stories. He obviously wants me to see him in a certain light; Wolfe has me meet him every morning at his opulent Tribeca loft, where he emerges from his bedroom with a different, much younger woman each day. He takes me to incredible dinners at the hippest restaurants in town, where everybody knows him. He has me accompany him to a board meeting for a charitable foundation, and he dominates the discussion, obviously performing for my benefit. He shows me a tape of his third wedding, where the guests include a staggering array of the world's most famous musicians, many of whom pay tribute to the great and powerful Wolfe. We attend a couple AA meetings together, where Wolfe goes on rants, hits on women, and introduces me around as "My Hollywood movie writer."

I grow quite fond of Wolfe, and I certainly relate to his drinking, drugging, and womanizing. I think Wolfe is fond of me too, especially the fact that I'm Jewish and sober. After an intense week together, Wolfe gives me his approval, and the green light to write his story.

I return to L.A. and write my ass off. This is the first screenplay I've written in a long while that is commissioned, and also something I'm actually interested in. I finish the script, and am encouraged by the positive response. Everybody is high on it. When a director comes on board, he (like many directors), decides that he is going to rewrite my script. He does so. In my opinion, his rewrite is a mess, but I don't share that take with anyone except Abe, who agrees, but just shrugs. The project makes the rounds, but nobody bites. Eventually, it dies. I am really pained, but powerless.

5 8
HOLLYWOOD ENDING

Abe sends me a script written by Nora, a woman he knows in New York. He says it's her first script, needs a rewrite, and he thought of me. I read Nora's script, which needs work, but she is clearly talented. I phone Nora, and we have a lengthy conversation about her script. I bring up the cost of a rewrite. Nora is flat broke, can't afford a penny. I've had my fill of pro bono work, and I pass on the re-write. Nora had read my script about Wolfe, and she's dying to meet him. I arrange for Wolfe and Nora to meet. They hit it off. Apparently, Nora is quite charismatic and attractive.

I tell Abe about Wolfe and Nora meeting, and his eyes light up, as his producer instinct kicks in; Abe thinks there's the potential for a great film here, a New York City, May-December romantic comedy with characters based on Wolfe and Nora. He thinks Nora and I should co-write it. We agree to do so, on spec, of course. It's an unusual partnership; Nora and I have never met, we live on opposite coasts, and we will have to write together via phone and email.

I've had difficult writing partnerships before; among them were an old friend, who, in the middle of writing a script together, turned into a raving, right-wing lunatic, a stand-up comedian who was great at pitching our ideas, but turned out to have zero interest in actually writing, and a producer I wrote with who smoked pot all day, everyday. I wrote with him for months, enveloped in a cloud of pot smoke (not recommended for the recovering alcoholic), and fearing I'd jeopardize the gig, I never said a word about it. One day, many months into the writing, the producer says to me, "Hey, man, does it bother you if I get high when we write?" I respond, "Actually, it kinda does." The producer tosses his joint out the window, "Sorry about that, man."

None of those partnerships come close to the torture of writing with Nora; she is exceedingly bright, articulate, and mercurial, and even though she's only written one script, Nora sees herself as a major showbiz figure, and she expects to be regarded as such. As we begin our collaboration, I discover, to my horror, that Nora is a nasty, abusive, paranoid narcissist who resents me and my writing experience, and is prone to hysteria. I find myself walking on egg shells. Her life is in utter disarray. She is constantly broke, and asks *me* for loans—that's rich.

The producers grow weary of Nora's prima donna act, and complain to *me*, as if I can do anything to control or change her.

The situation becomes so unpleasant, I find myself speaking with Stephan much more than I usually do, just to stay sane. Whatever serenity I once had is blown to bits, but I choose to remain in the partnership, hoping that the results will justify the unpleasantness.

Nora is obsessed with power and control. As we near the end of our first draft, she has her lawyer make a threatening phone call to me; in a tough guy voice, he informs me that if there is a re-write, "his client" should write it alone, and that the original contract needs to be revised to give Nora the lion's share of the fee. This is preposterous, and I let the lawyer know that. I never hear from him again, but the experience is unnerving.

We finish the script, and miraculously, it turns out great. Everybody loves it, including Abe's Creative Artists agents who set up a reading, with Robert De Niro and Jennifer Aniston playing the lead roles. This is what many writers dream of; to hear their words spoken by talented actors. But the producers feel that Nora cannot attend the reading; their fear is that Nora will act out, and behave in such a way that threatens the project. Unfortunately, this means that I (as Nora's partner), also will not attend. Of course, Nora can't know this, so I am tasked with coming up with a bogus reason for why the writers can't attend the reading.

I am told later that the reading went quite well, but afterward, there is precious little forward movement. The producers say the script is great, but not great enough, and they ask Nora and me to go back to the drawing board. Again, I allow Nora back into my life, and I pay the price. A writing relationship is almost as intimate as a marriage, and it is impossible to not be affected by your partner. I feel like a hostage, albeit, a willing one.

In the midst of Nora's and my rewriting, a director is attached, and he is *paid* to do a rewrite. His rewrite doesn't work. Nora and I are asked to do a rewrite of the directors rewrite of our script. I can't say no, but I wish I did. The experience of having her in my life so intimately is soul-crushing. Over time, the original actors leave the project, new hi-profile actors and directors are attached, then unattached, and eventually, the producers curtail their efforts, and they move on to other projects. The lengthy, torturous slog to get the movie made fizzles.

I am beat, and beaten. Another huge investment of time, and nothing to show for it. On this one, I left too much of myself on the field. The combination of years in the Hollywood sausage-grinder, and now, Hurricane Nora, has completely gutted me. I have nobody to blame but myself; I had reached a moment of such desperation and need that I was willing to do anything. I betrayed myself and lost my way. I accepted the unacceptable. It was a gamble, one that I lost, and one that sucked the life out of me. It becomes hard to respect myself. I can no longer live like this.

59
HUNTING HEADS

The writing is on the wall, so to speak, my showbiz career is over; twenty-five years of frustration, financial insecurity, self-torture, and if I'm honest, quite a lot of fun. It's painful to walk away. Being a writer-director has been such a major part of my identity. I've had the opportunity to be creative for many years, and I've enjoyed some nice paydays. But, I finally reach a point where I am no longer willing to fight; slugging it out in the trenches, dealing with abusive personalities, feeling the desperation, neediness and instability, and finally, the reality that I can no longer make a viable living in this business. I wave the white flag of surrender. And as I discovered with my foreclosure, an awful, painful situation can turn out, over time, to be a blessing.

An old friend of mine, Todd, also a friend of Bill, and an ex-stand-up comedian who left the biz long ago, is now a wildly successful corporate executive search professional. Todd has been bugging me for years to leave "Hollywood's cannibalistic culture" and come work with him, as a headhunter. I've always declined; I have zero interest in corporate anything. But, I've reached a moment where my interests take a distant back seat to being self-supporting. I contact Todd who is happy to hire me, and thrilled to have been right about my career. Todd is a twisted but funny guy. We've attended meetings together, collaborated on off-color song lyrics, and co-created an original web series about life in sobriety, called *Restless, Irritable, and Discontented*.

At first, I can't stand the headhunting job; I'm terribly uncomfortable on the phone, worried that these high-level execs will realize I know nothing about their business, or even business in general. I spend each day bracing for the moment when I will be revealed as a fraud. Initially, there isn't a single creative thing about the job, unless you count color-coding the files. Todd doesn't have the patience to train me at all. It's sink or swim. I feel the familiar pang of abandonment, but I remind myself that I'm an adult now, not a child, and I'm committed to making this work. I can't afford to listen to my head. Todd as a friend is fine, but as a boss, it's another story. He suffers (so I suffer) from his A.D.D, A.D.H.D., severe narcissism, *and* he insists that I listen to all the new jokes he writes.

I have always been uncomfortable with anything I'm not instantly good at, or anything that represents change. But, I force myself to focus on the positives of this new job; I get to work from home, my age doesn't matter, and I don't have to perform dog and pony shows for executive approval. I start to loosen up and have fun with the gig; I do different voices on the phone to get past gate-keepers, and I get a kick being on the phone with big-time CEOs, while I'm in the nude. On business calls, I still have no idea what I'm talking about, but I toss out big words, try to sound authoritative, and no one ever accuses me of being a phony.

More than anything, the job provides a sense of stability, and a peace I've never experienced. That desperate, needy feeling is a thing of the past. My income is healthy and steady, and erases the financial insecurity that has plagued me most of my adult life. After decades of a roller coaster existence, I discover the simple satisfaction of having a regular old job. Poppy sees the changes in me and my life, and she couldn't be more supportive and delighted. I'm surprised how very much that means to me.

60

THE THREE OF US

Poppy invites me to join her and Char on a trip to England. It feels so nice to be included, but at the same time, I'm nervous to meet her family. What if they don't like me? Or see through me? Maybe they've never met a Jew before. Poppy's parents have passed away, but she has seven siblings, who will all be at the restaurant where we will meet.

It's an unusually warm day in London, and that, in addition to my anxiety causes me to break out in a flop sweat as we get lost trying to find the restaurant. Finally, we arrive. Char turns to me and says, "Yuck, you're all wet!" Indeed, my shirt is soaked. I panic, I need to find a way to get out of this situation, but Poppy pushes me into the restaurant, where we are greeted by a gang of smiling, ruddy, red-haired siblings. I am embraced by these strangers, none of whom seem to mind my moisture. Sitting at the table, I initially feel like Woody Allen in the scene from *Annie Hall*, where he imagines that Diane

Keaton's white bread family sees him as an Ultra-Orthodox Jew. But, all of Poppy's siblings could not be more incredibly warm. They make me feel like family.

Poppy and I have been together for over two years now, and we are almost always at each other's apartment. Char isn't nearly as vocal as she used to be about her objections to my presence. It occurs to me that we should maybe think about getting a place of our own, the three of us. Poppy concurs.

We look at a bunch of houses, always with Char, who isn't exactly loving this "Unvoluntary uprootment," as Char calls it. We find a funky old Spanish place, we move in, and begin to make it a home. Poppy and I each have two cats, who luxuriate around the house, until we acquiesce to Char's desire to get a dog, prompting the cats to start living on the highest shelves, coming down only when the dog is asleep.

The humans are faring a little better, although, since we've all moved in together, Char makes it clear that she is not entirely sold on me; when I drive her to school, and try to make conversation, she says, "I don't like talking in a moving vehicle." My approach to Char, based on advice from Stephan, is to just be there, consistently, no pressure, no demands, no imposing my will. Char will come around if and when she does. Then one day, an opening—Char loves movies, and asks me to show her how to write a screenplay. She even deigns to allow me to help her write one, on the subject of grammar school witches.

The other significant young lady in my life, my niece Lexie, chooses to spend some of her vacations with us. My sister, Amy, allows Lexie, now a teenager, to travel here alone. I'm so touched that Amy trusts me with her daughter. There were years when no one in my family allowed me to be alone with any of their children. Lexie is a free spirit, a socially conscious, budding activist, and an all-state water polo player. Char is fascinated with Lexie, and enjoys having an older girl to hang with. Poppy adores Lexie, and our animals can't keep their paws off of her. Lexie is not an alcoholic, but she loves going to AA meetings with me. She enjoys hearing the grisly stories, and mingling with the drunks. Lexie becomes a kind of mascot at the meetings, and when she goes back home, all the alcoholics ask me where she is.

For the first time in long while, or maybe ever, I live in a place that feels like a home. The people and animals I live with feel like family. And, for the first time in memory, I actually feel at peace most of the time. That's not to say I'm perfect. "Flawed, clueless, selfish, thoughtless, fucked up, and *totally* fucked up" are words Poppy uses to describe me when my behavior or attitude is less than desirable. She will absolutely not put up with any of my crap, and she comes down hard on me when I mess up. I admire her strength, and am amazed that someone can be so soft and so hard at the same time.

Acceptance is one of the most discussed topics in meetings, with the emphasis on accepting the *negative*. These days, I'm finding it harder to accept the *positives* in my life—a loving relationship, happy home, financial security, good health, long-time sobriety, and the joy of sponsoring guys who trust me. Do I deserve to have this? When will my luck run out? How soon will all of this be taken away? I have always had a negative orientation—rejection, disappointment, loss, and fear, are what I'm most familiar and comfortable with. Those feelings are what I naturally focus on, and give weight to. If twenty people read a script I've written, and nineteen people love it, I only pay attention to the one person who doesn't love it. These days, in my mind, a tug-of-war rages, in which I try to stay positive, while fighting off the foreboding sense of waiting for the other shoe to drop. But it doesn't drop. The shoe stays on the foot.

61

IT'S RARE, MAN

Along with my intense fear of becoming just like my father, I've also lived with the certainty that I should never *be* a father. But the longer I'm sober, the more I'm able to let go of old ideas, and the idea that I'm destined to be a bad dad just because my dad was one, has finally evaporated. My relationships with Char and Lexie contribute greatly to my belief that I could be a decent father. Since I met Poppy, I've experienced a powerful and growing desire to have a child. Oddly, I have never discussed this with Poppy, but I know we have to talk about it soon, given that I've decided to ask her to marry me.

I make a dinner reservation at a pricey seafood restaurant in Malibu. I've jumped the gun a tad, with an engagement ring tucked in my pocket. Poppy orders a glass of wine, and I wish I could too. She looks at me with concern.

"Are you okay? You're white as a ghost."

"I'm fine. A little carsick. Mostly glad to just hang out, talk a little."

"Why here?"

"It's a nice restaurant, and you love seafood."

"*You* don't."

"I just can't handle the bones, even when they say no bones, I find bones."

"So you brought me here to talk about fish bones?"

"No, I want to talk about something else."

Poppy waits. I just sit there.

"And that something *is*…?" Poppy eventually asks.

I clear my throat, a couple of times, working up the nerve.

"Okay, the thing is, I've spent my whole life thinking that I would be a lousy father, because…"

"I know."

"Well, I don't feel that way anymore. Finally, at forty-five."

"That's wonderful."

"What I'm doing a really lousy job of saying is…I'd like to have a baby…with you…And, you know, be your husband."

Silence. Poppy appears to be in pain. This isn't the response I expected.

"Wow, I'm sorry I brought that up," I say.

"No, it's good that you did."

"Could have fooled me."

"Sweetheart, I love you. I couldn't love you more. But having a baby…I'm forty-two years old…"

"Some woman in Africa just gave birth at sixty."

"It's not about giving birth, it's about raising a child. I've done that. It was the most wonderful experience of my life. I just don't want to don't want to go through it again, not at this point in my life."

"I got it."

"You're upset."

"I'm not upset."

I'm crushed. She cries. The ring stays in my pocket.

In a confused and emotional state, I describe my dilemma to Stephan; I want to marry Poppy, and I desperately long to be a father, but I can't have both.

"That's a tough one," he ponders, "I can't make the decision for you."

A long pause, then…

"I ever tell you about that guy, Frank, the landscape architect?"

"I don't think so."

"Fucking beautiful man, inside and out. Really loved him. We wanted to be together, but he had to move to Boston. His mom was real sick. I didn't want to move, I needed to be here, where I could get "discovered." So, we broke up. I never did fall in love again…that was over thirty years ago…It's rare, man."

6 2

MAZEL TOV

Our wedding is held at Cousin Buzz's sprawling home outside L.A., in horse country. Poppy's relatives come from England, mine from Chicago. And friends from everywhere. Half the guests get drunk, half don't. Poppy looks gorgeous, like a more attractive Grace Kelly. Officiating at the ceremony is my old pal and star of *Ice Cream Man*, Roman, who has become some kind of ordained minister. Cousin Johan performs a beautiful solo guitar rendition of *Love Theme from Spartacus*. In a bit of a surprise, Char dances with me, her feet on my shoes. My aunt Carolyn, who is deliriously happy for me, takes me aside, to lavish praise on Poppy, "Oh, Duffy, your bride is so lovely and sweet and charming and warm and decent...nothing *at all* like your mother." Ah, family.

Toasts are delivered by well-wishers; Cousin Buzz leads it off, welcoming everyone to a day no one ever thought would happen. My three sisters and Lexie team up for a hilarious toast, a roast really, in which they savage me, in the most loving way. Poppy's brother, Dicky gives a heartfelt tribute to his sister. Abe weighs in, with harrowing tales from our childhood. Then Abe's eleven-year-old son, my godson, Ely, takes the stage, proclaiming that *The Godfather* is his godfather's favorite movie, and he repeats the words of Luca Brazzi, "May your first child be a masculine child." Finally, I cap it off by making a toast, *voluntarily*...when I have to speak in public, I usually can't wait to get off the stage. Today, I could talk forever. And I do. A couple guests nod off. After I finish, Stephan gives me a kiss on the cheek, and whispers...

"You done good, kid."

"Thanks, I felt pretty comfortable up there."

Stephan shakes his head.

"I'm not talking about your fucking speech, I'm talking about your fucking *life*."

I let that sink in—I feel pretty fucking good.

63

EPILOGUE

As I write this, at the ripe old age of sixty-three, Poppy and I have been married for eighteen amazingly harmonious years, and I've been sober for thirty-three. A few years ago, Poppy relocated us from L.A. to Ojai, a small town surrounded by mountains, a couple of hours north. Our life here can best be described as "serene," a word I've always gagged on (but now embrace). Another word I've had trouble with in the past is "gratitude." But how can I *not* be grateful for over thirty years of life beyond my likely expiration date. For freedom from the tyrannical demons that plagued my entire existence. For a comfort in my own skin that I never thought possible.

I enjoy a relatively simple, quiet life. No longer consumed with the need to possess the toys and trappings of success, I've given up the pursuit of fabulousness that I inherited from my parents, which was always connected to the belief that something on the outside could fix what's wrong on the inside. It took me a lifetime to become my own man, but I think that finally, I'm him.

The female foot (other than Poppy's) barely has an impact on me any longer, but I do stay away from the ballet.

After having accepted the reality that I was never going to experience fatherhood, in the most unexpected twist of my life—and just in time for her adolescence—Char decided I wasn't such a bad guy after all, and she allowed me fully into her life. This opened the door to what has become the most deeply fulfilling relationship.

My nephew Sammy, the one whose curiosity inspired this book, is currently in a rehab facility, dealing with alcohol and drug issues. Sammy and I talk all the time. I couldn't identify more strongly with him—I *was* him. As much as I want to rescue Sammy, that is not possible. I can only pray that he finds the freedom I've found. During a recent phone call, echoing Sammy's initial question to me, I ask him, "Why do you think you drink?" Sammy says, "It's a long story." I respond, "I've got all day."

The last couple of decades have been relatively drama-free for Poppy and me, with one profoundly significant exception: on January 17, 2014, our niece, Lexie, who was living in Afghanistan, where she was helping to educate young women, was murdered, at the age of twenty-seven, by the Taliban.

Words cannot express the shock and the loss. Lexie was such an extraordinary young woman, and so beloved, with incredible promise. Her way-too-short life was devoted to improving the lives of others less fortunate, first in African villages, then in Afghanistan. Often, when people pass away, they are deified, but Lexie was truly a goddess. Her tragic death was, and is, absolutely devastating, an unthinkable horror that broke the hearts and shattered the lives of everyone in our family. I have to admit, when I heard about what happened to Lexie, the thought of drinking entered my mind, as did the thought of violent revenge, but no action was taken on either front. I worried that my sister, Lexie's mom, Amy, would not be able to survive the wrenching loss of her only child. Since Lexie's death, and to this day, I phone Amy every Sunday. I listen, and I try to provide comfort, but I don't know if that's even possible.

The day before Lexie's funeral, the rabbi spoke with Amy, Liza, Jewel, and me, to hear our stories and remembrances about Lexie, so that her eulogy could be more personal. Among other things, I talked about how Lexie attended AA meetings with me, and how much everyone there loved her.

Lexie's murder had been well publicized in the Chicago media, and an overflow crowd of more than four hundred people showed up for her funeral, in addition to lots of press. In the middle of her eulogy, the rabbi mentions that Lexie attended my AA meetings with me. My sister, Jewel, sitting next me, is outraged, "That rabbi just outed you, in front of *everyone*." I shrug. Jewel fumes, "Doesn't that bother you?" "Not really," I whisper. This day isn't about me. And I am no longer a keeper of secrets. It's been a very long time since I had even the slightest trace of embarrassment or shame about being an alcoholic. In the words of Popeye the Sailor Man, "I yam what I yam."

As far as *who* I am, I've devoted years to trying to figure that out, and I still don't really know. At this point, I don't think about it much. What I do know is that I have learned an awful lot I didn't know before, lessons that have saved and dramatically improved my life; I have learned how to have a healthy, intimate relationship with another person, how to love, how to help, how to listen, how to show up, how to forgive, how to look beyond myself.

I have learned that it's okay to ask for help, that love is an action, that I am not alone, that feelings aren't facts, that there exists a gray area between perfection and worthlessness, that laughter is as essential as oxygen, that my life doesn't work if I am my own higher power. I have learned how to live remarkably comfortably with a number of potentially debilitating addictions.

I have had an enormous amount of help along the way, from the most wonderful, wise, and patient teachers...My sponsor,

Stephan, died of a heart attack some years ago, but I continue to honor our agreement from the first time we met, "We do not drink, we do not use, one day at a time, *no matter what.*"

ACKNOWLEDGMENTS

For their invaluable support, wisdom, guidance, and love, and without whom there would be no Blotto, I want to express my heartfelt gratitude to Poosy Holmes, Gigi Braybrooks, Ali Pohn, Jack McCarthy, Brian Levant, Alison Logan-Levant, Mitch Sisskind, Liz Dubelman, Stanley Kamel, and Merl Edelman.

Made in the USA
San Bernardino, CA
21 April 2020